ANYW...

ANU VAIDYANATHAN is the founder of PatNMarks, an intellectual property consulting firm. Anu received her PhD in electrical engineering at UC Canterbury, setting the department and university record in twenty-six months. She has been teaching courses in computer architecture, innovation and business policy at the Indian Institute of Technology, Ropar, and the Indian Institute of Management, Ahmedabad.

Anu is a regular speaker at forums on entrepreneurship, innovation and leadership. She is also an endurance athlete representing India in long-course triathlon. She became the first Asian female to have competed in the Ultraman Canada triathlon, comprising a 10-km swim, a 420-km bike ride and an 84.4-km run. She backed this up with Ironman Canada comprising a 3.8-km swim, a 180-km bike ride and a 42.2-km run, four weeks later.

ANYWHERE BUT HOME

Adventures in Endurance

ANU VAIDYANATHAN

Harper
Sport

First published in India in 2016 by Harper Sport
An imprint of HarperCollins *Publishers*

Copyright © Anu Vaidyanathan 2016

P-ISBN: 978-93-5177-524-9
E-ISBN: 978-93-5177-525-6

2 4 6 8 10 9 7 5 3 1

Anu Vaidyanathan asserts the moral right
to be identified as the author of this work.

The views and opinions expressed in this book are the author's own and the facts are
as reported by her, and the publishers are not in any way liable for the same.

HarperCollins *Publishers*
A-75, Sector 57, Noida, Uttar Pradesh 201301, India
1 London Bridge Street, London, SE1 9GF, United Kingdom
Hazelton Lanes, 55 Avenue Road, Suite 2900, Toronto, Ontario M5R 3L2
and 1995 Markham Road, Scarborough, Ontario M1B 5M8, Canada
25 Ryde Road, Pymble, Sydney, NSW 2073, Australia
195 Broadway, New York, NY 10007, USA

Typeset in 11/14 Adobe Devanagari
by Jojy Philip, New Delhi 110 015

Printed and bound at
Thomson Press (India) Ltd

For Ashish
My special place in your heart,
my darling, is the home that I was chosen for.

Contents

Prologue

Heartbreak after swimming 10 km, riding 420 km and running more than 60 km would be the worst. I felt a nagging sense of desperation as I squinted through my sunglasses, trying to see the road. My eyes were stinging from the salt running into them. There was not a spot of shade anywhere. For the first time in three days, I was not sure I could finish the last stage of Ultraman Canada, an endurance race that less than five hundred people in the world had completed. As a handful of competitors swam, biked and ran through the edge of the Okanagan Desert in British Columbia, the semi-arid steppe seemed determined to extract the last morsel of self-pity out of all of us.

I was a PhD student in electrical and computer engineering at the University of Canterbury in Christchurch, New Zealand. As an athlete, I had trained and raced in Bangalore, Chennai, Mumbai, Manali, Christchurch, Queenstown, Auckland, Melbourne, Seattle, Alaska, Orlando, Brazil, Ottawa and Montreal, among other places. I had discovered my mythical wishbone and honed it with miles of practice, over and over again, till it shone that day in the bright Canadian sun. Quitting was not an option.

I had never considered the odds of finishing Ultraman Canada till I got to the start line. I had trained at an altitude for many weeks, in Park City, Utah, and felt a great kinship with the prospectors who had crowded to the silver mines there. Turned out, I was looking for my sliver of silver on this expedition with my body and my mind.

Being a self-supported race, the Ultraman required athletes to have a crew. Mine had been put together by some helpful people trying to get me to the finish line. I liked Lori, my one-person swim-crew, the moment I met her. She was amazingly positive, this complete stranger so surprisingly invested in my success. But my glee was short-lived. By the third day, when we started the double marathon, my race-crew was no longer by my side. After 50 km, I had asked them to step aside. Somehow, I had started to feel like a science experiment and Lori was outnumbered by the two other crew members who were not exactly encouraging. I just knew I had to do the last 30-odd kilometres of running by myself.

POLYAMORY

Crossroads

Freedom is just another word for nothing left to lose.
                                        —*Me and Bobby McGee,* Janis Joplin

A light rain had started to fall. The journey back to Madison was taking longer than I had thought it would. Driving 1,600 km in two days had been the plan, to give myself some time to think after running a ten-miler – aptly called the Hangover Classic – on the last day of 2004. Driving through a storm, zipping through West Virginia across the Appalachians, watching dark grey clouds tease the distance between them and my rear-view mirror, I heard the windshield wipers turning on. They sounded like the second hand of a giant clock, ticking away. My bike was nestled in the backseat of the car along with my minimal baggage. Within minutes, the skies opened up. The clouds had caught up with me.

Soul Asylum's '*Runaway train*' was playing on the radio, a morbid reminder that I needed to keep my eye on the highway, which was barely visible, to avoid getting completely lost. The heating was broken and the windshield was fogging up. Every few seconds, I would lean forward and wipe the glass with my hand. It was raining heavily, but then again, in some ways, it had not stopped raining for three years.

My rental car was called Sal, named after the great Sal Paradise, and like a best friend should, it seemed to be propelling me towards my reckoning. Back then, it was fashionable to read Jack Kerouac and laugh at the antics of the crazy Dean Moriarty, whose knock on the door you waited for, much like you might wait for the moonlight to throw its magic on some secret corner you had never noticed before, while on a bike ride through the night. I had a boyfriend who was a lot like Dean Moriarty. A triathloning, All-American version, but crazy like Dean. And spontaneous. I think I was in love. You would have to be, with a boy who took you on an 13-km run through the woods on your first date. He and I and our friends at college usually ran, biked and swam several kilometres in the early hours of the morning, before most others woke up. We were a motley crew of runners, cyclists and triathletes, some nutcases even participating in the Ironman Triathlon – the longest single-day triathlon in the world, with a 3.8-km swim, 180-km bike ride, 42.2-km run, and a time-limit of seventeen hours for completion. I didn't take the triathletes too seriously then, choosing instead to ride my bike, fondly named Zippy, and explore new places for hours on end, without spending on petrol. Zippy and I were fast friends and sweat seemed a worthy substitute for more sedentary pursuits like television.

During Christmas in 2004, I was visiting some friends in Raleigh, and one evening we went out to catch the screening of a new video game at an animation show. We were drinking Coca-Cola and eating chips, the staple diet for engineering students. The game clip showed a man with longish hair, who seemed to have no time for a haircut because he was too busy chasing through the landscape, searching long and hard for something. He reminded me of a cloud I had seen when I first arrived in Madison: it had shot across the sky in one seemingly never ending sentence. The man in the clip stopped at an abyss, nowhere left to go, and sighed. You could see his shoulders droop, not like he had given up, but in a sort of questioning way, as though wondering, 'What now?' I identified with his question, because after studying in five colleges, living in six cities and spending six years in America, feverishly chasing daydreams, I had reached the end of my tether.

On the surface, it seemed like I had it all. I was in one of the most coveted PhD programmes at the University of Wisconsin in Madison. It had been my dream to get there and when I finally did, it took many months for it to feel real. I was working with the rock stars of academic research. That they occasionally stared at my chest during late-night meetings was just a detail in my head. That they did not pay me for my work, although I was more qualified than my male peers and often worked longer hours than their paid staff, was another detail. That I suddenly missed my parents every single day, after several years of forgetting birthdays and anniversaries, and wasn't happy going to work for the first time in my life – that was not just a detail. It was a real problem.

I did not love my job or my circumstances, but I did not want to give up quickly. I was in a blossoming relationship. I had the best of friends. Yet, I was unable to fit in and could not understand why I was depressed. The thought of moving back to Bangalore seemed to carry the undeniable stamp of failure. I dreaded going home. My father had faced ample criticism for letting an eighteen-year-old girl pursue a degree abroad. I was the quintessential Tamilian Brahmin – five times a year at least, during Pongal, Nombu, Ganapathi Chaturthi, Krishna Jayanti and Deepavali; I found M.S. Subbulakshmi and the Red Hot Chilli Peppers equally appealing. It scandalized my aunts to no end that I watched *Sex and the City* uncensored. Truth was, I looked forward just as much to borrowing the latest Tamil or Hindi VCD making the rounds amongst friends who had returned from their yearly trips to India. I revered Thoreau and Thiruvalluvar equally. And my identity found kinship with a small menagerie demonstrating similar conflicting impulses.

Back in Madison, a few weeks later, I scoped the entire route advertised for the Mad City Marathon, and tacked on an hour-long run at the end of it, lost in thought. It was deep in the winter and the last hour found me on the shores of Lake Mendota. Hell seemed to have literally frozen over, into a bleak white sheet of ice. I had stopped briefly, without knowing why. After the daze of blood rushing all over had faded and the world became clear, for an infinitesimal period of time, I thought I saw a lone duck making its way gingerly across the lake. Was it a hallucination, or had I finally seen the elusive Shingebiss, a hardy duck according to Ojibwa folklore. The Ojibwa were one group of Native Americans or Paleo-Indians or Red Indians, whatever one wanted to call the indigenous dwellers of the land. It was Shingebiss

who famously said, 'Adapt or perish.' Maybe this duck was only part
legend, I thought in my depleted state. Maybe those words of wisdom
struck home to more than the Ojibwa; they made perfect sense to me,
even though I belonged to the *other* group of Indians.

A few months later, I quit my PhD and bought a one-way ticket
to India.

After flying into Bangalore from Madison via Chicago and Frankfurt,
I slept for two hours in my parents' house and then went for a run at
5.30 a.m. that very morning. On that run, I realized that life had
changed in ways I would never completely fathom, but the key to
understanding was to keep my heart open. When I stepped onto our
street, which is lined with two rows of houses set 20 feet apart, it was
bathed in a pale orange light from the street lamps. The lights that
burned in the individual houses broke the pattern of the convex circles
of streetlight, as if to rebel against the monochrome uniformity of it all.
As my feet hit the tarred roads in our rather sleepy neighbourhood of
Basaveshwaranagar, I was aware of being alone. My sports bra obscured
my assets a bit, but the nose-ring gleaming under the streetlights was a
dead giveaway. Within a kilometre or so, I sensed I was being followed,
but I brushed it aside as jet-lag and disorientation caused by the sudden
onslaught of headlights from a speeding car. A few more minutes and
I heard heavy panting, but it seemed to originate from a height lower
than my own. I turned around and, to my horror, saw half a dozen
dogs jogging behind me. I did not make eye contact. I did not try to
run faster. I was afraid, but I kept calm because I had no choice. I was
wearing long pants so I knew that even if I got bitten, I had one level
of protection.

I was reminded then of an incident on a road trip with my maternal
grandmother, Mangalam-paati, when we were touring some temples
in south India during our summer vacation in the early 1990s.
Since it was a pilgrimage of sorts, every temple town we passed, my
grandmother would tell us a story about the deity there and pay her
respects by touching both her cheeks with her right hand and praying.
My grandmother loved to sing. She would sing between stops in

the mini-van that all my cousins, their parents and my parents were piled into. My uncles jokingly tried to get her to stop, but she stuck to her guns because her grandkids were enjoying singing along. At a traffic light, one of my uncles suddenly exclaimed, 'Amma, *Bhairavar vahanam ma,*' in response to which my grandmother stopped singing and quickly paid her respects, only to realize in a second that my uncle had been pulling her leg. *Bhairavar vahanam* referred to a humble dog that was standing by the roadside, looking at the passing traffic. My grandmother laughed, smacked my uncle, and said that all animals were worth praying to and singing for. After which, she continued to sing. I looked back at my own followers on my morning run in Bangalore once more and decided that, if chased or followed by a pack of dogs while running, it was best to not run faster or have a heart-attack. In fact, it was best to sing to them silently and stay calm.

As I approached Malleswaram bridge, the group had changed and a different set of dogs had joined me. I began to wonder how much longer they would follow me. The number of cars, cycles and pedestrians seemed to multiply once I crossed the Windsor Manor bridge. If the dogs were jogging as a relay team, I was sure I would lose the race to them, even though my longest run until that morning had been around five hours, somewhere in America. I was starting to giggle just a little, wondering whether I would end up running a marathon right after a crazy journey. Then I burst into laughter, thinking: 'Forget marathons, I am going to do a whole Ironman, swim 3.8 km, bike 180 km and run 42.2 km, dogs or no dogs!' I entertained that thought over the next hour of running. When I finished, I asked myself, 'Am I doing this for fun?' The answer came almost immediately. 'Hell, no! I am doing this to buy me my oblivion.'

Counterculture

Timshel, Thou mayest

—*East of Eden*, John Steinbeck

In early 2005, the three spoken words that often made me break into a cold sweat were, *Wanna get coffee?* Coffee shops were an epidemic across Bangalore, as were Lance Armstrong's yellow wristbands. Why anyone would want to spend ten times the money for a hot beverage in an air-conditioned coffee shop rather than drinking coffee at a local eatery was beyond me. Wearing a piece of plastic on one's wrist when daytime temperatures mandated the use of deodorant was even more incomprehensible. I had left Bangalore to study in America when I was eighteen and returned seven years later, only to find that time-travel was indeed possible, even on Air India. I felt I had been gone for over twenty years.

Being an engineer, I spoke almost exclusively in *Star Wars* analogies, often inducing puzzled looks on the faces of my more amorous coffee-buyers. I thought it was normal to encourage people by saying, 'May the Force be with you!' Perhaps what they really expected from me was that I hold their hand, lean in and say something different, if at all. I was unaware for many moons that being 'foreign-returned' meant that I was considered to be eligible to those who could afford expensive coffee. I had been a scholarship student most of my life and held jobs that required me to wash dishes, stock shelves, teach classes or write code outside of my college work for at least twenty hours a week. I considered myself the kind of blue-collar girl who drank beer out of a bottle, not a chilled glass. The air-conditioning soon got on my nerves and I stopped drinking coffee and beer altogether.

I had convinced my parents to allow me to stay by myself – that had been our agreement on my moving back. I did not want to be a cranky roommate and my own space offered me a chance to keep my old life in America intact, as much as I could.

I spent most of my working hours setting up a small business in Bangalore with the help of my brother. We worked out of an office housed in a windowless basement – for someone who loved sunshine, this was a harsh dose of reality. When the monsoons arrived a month later, the first day of torrential rain flooded the entire office. Since the entrance was on an incline, the water was going to come in, no matter what. The outside drainage had clogged up and what unfolded was a character-defining experience. My brother and I sent the staff home, rolled up our shirts and pants, got on the floor and started mopping. There was never any discussion about what needed to be done. With the help of a broomstick, the drainage was also unclogged. When we sat down to dinner that night, my brother and I grinned at each other, as if it was our own little joke. We both preferred to strike out on our own, even if it meant mopping floors.

We would stay in that office for seven years to come, and it was the best office of all. If you asked me why, I'd tell you that it was because it taught two city brats that dreams are not built on fresh air and sunshine alone, and because it embodied everything a small business should. I quickly started acquiring new clients from among the abundant technology startups in Bangalore and stopped asking American-educated questions such as *Can I get some bottled water?*

Starting a business in India in 2005 was a tiring prospect. We named the company PatNMarks and positioned ourselves as a product company building prior-art search databases for Indian IP information. I had graduated with a bachelor's and master's in computer engineering and writing computer programmes was really all that I knew how to do. Building a search-engine to work with an antiquated database seemed like a really cool problem to solve. Just as most of my cherished trinkets come from my mother, so did this idea. She explained to me that searching for information on any patent, trademark, or other intellectual property filed in India was not an easy, automated task. It involved physical visits to patent offices in the metros and hours of sifting through files. She outlined the problem simply enough for me to jump in head first, ready to tackle it in the best way I could. It did not ruffle or embarrass me that my initial funding came from my father. I felt empowered and humbled by the fact that he believed in me and supported my decisions. My father has fended for himself since he was seventeen. He had also built a successful business, along with my mother. Even if I did not enjoy it or agree with it at times, I listened to my father's advice keenly. I resisted the urge to rent a building and buy myself a grand desk, as the capital we had was better spent on more important things, such as setting up a website and hiring people.

The Bangalore I had returned to was just not the same place I had left behind. I tried reconnecting with my childhood friends, but I found that I didn't understand them anymore. Most were married and had their own families to attend to. A lot of things in life came easy for many of us; our parents owned homes, we had hired help when we needed it, babies were washed, cleaned and burped by someone else and laundry was a heavenly non-chore. Staying in touch with my friends in the US was proving difficult; we did not have smartphones yet. My best friend from college and I tried to stay in touch via email and phone calls, which cost a pretty penny. On one particularly long call, he told me that his groovy girlfriend of many years had left him. He was sobbing on the phone while I tried to convince him to turn to David Sedaris instead of other forms of stress relief. We recalled a famous line from his audio CDs, all the rage before I left America, in which he talks of his brother's attitude towards adversity: '*Shit man, when shit gets you down, just say "F-it" and eat yerself some candy!*' I felt terribly alone and helpless that day. I wanted to ape the good things about my time in America, riding bikes, thinking freely, seeking out friendships that lasted. My humanness seemed to be up for constant evaluation, but when my best friend misheard that as *Hanuman-ness*, I realized a little re-organization of letters was all it might take to convert my quandary into a vision of heroism, of a monkey-faced god carrying Sita's belongings out of burning Lanka.

Glimpse

Who in the world am I? Ah, that's the great puzzle.

—*Alice in Wonderland*, Lewis Carroll

I had grown into a woman in America. I was more individualistic than I cared to admit. I could not fit in anywhere. Not in America, not in Bangalore. Sport was my guiding light. My release. My excuse for not dealing with the more pressing facts as reiterated by people I no longer understood. Maybe I never understood them to begin with. Sport was slowly but surely starting to fill the void that culture and people could not fill. Life in India was as alienating as life in the US. Home was just geography at the end of the day.

While keeping my habits intact in Bangalore, I also tried finding ways to swim, bike and run, as I was used to doing in Madison. Training in all three disciplines in India requires imagination – one has to be able to imagine success before struggling with huge doses of inconvenient reality. At first, I went to a local pool in Bangalore where I was told that the entry fee was a few hundred rupees and that 'ladies' would only be able to swim between 3 p.m. and 4 p.m. It was my first introduction to a new reality, having to swim separately from the men. I dressed modestly, donning biking shorts and a t-shirt for my first swim. The water was extremely polluted, the lines were long, the lifeguards were absent, the dressing room was in shambles and the stench of urine was overpowering. Unsettled as I was, my need to swim was greater than anything else and I refused to be sidetracked. But a huge surprise awaited me in the pool. The 50-metre pool was closed and the 25-metre pool had a lane line drawn horizontally across, effectively making it a 12.5-metre pool. Most of the women were flailing about or relaxing at the wall, as if they were at a Turkish bath. Past the kerfuffle over lane-length, I got in and out in 30 minutes, swimming diagonally to maximize the length of my lap. As soon as I was out, I marched straight into the coach's office. When I passionately presented my case for women swimming in the 25-metre pool, he said, 'In all these years, you are the only woman who has ever asked for this. I don't see the need for it. It's unnecessary.' I knew that this man was a reputed coach and initially wondered if he was trying to test me in some way. I asked him whether I could join his 5.30 a.m. sessions with the team, as that would allow me to swim in the 50-metre pool. He asked me how old I was. When I said I was twenty-four, his casual but immediate response was, 'Swimming-*alla yakamma – madve maadkoli.*' (Not worth it. Give up swimming. Get married.) To hear such a derogatory and unbelievably stupid statement from a man who was supposedly an accomplished coach inflamed me. I realized I needed to get away from all this negativity, so I started sneaking into private pools at the high-rises that were slowly beginning to dot the landscape of Bangalore. It was pretty easy to slip into these buildings. Putting down a fictional flat number usually worked with the guards and visiting an imaginary aunt was an easier sell. I spoke Kannada quite well, had a nose-ring and probably looked harmless. It was harder in the winters because most of the pools were outdoors and not heated. I tried getting into an exclusive club, but their membership fee was equivalent to a whole year's salary, and then some. And I was too proud to ask my father for the money.

I had started riding my bike very early in the morning. Given my lack of social life, I was up by 4 a.m. and out on the road by 4.45. Very often, I would hear the *Suprabhatam* on a neighbour's radio or tape-recorder. Though this is the song that wakes many south Indian households, I never quite understood the words until I wrote this book.

> O Rāma, the noble son of Kausalyā! The Sandhyā of the East commences. O lion amongst men! Arise, the daily tasks are to be performed. (1.23.2)

In protecting my mornings, I was awakening to a life of duty. The
sights that greeted me every morning lifted my spirits; the smell of a
freshly washed porch, women stooped over their colourful rangolis,
coupled with the fresh morning air was invigorating. Riding around
the streets of Bangalore early in the morning was like being in a
monochrome disco. Orange street lamp, patch of black, orange street
lamp, patch of black. The rhythm from this disco was mostly between
my ears. Once I left the residential areas, the roads were lit with
differing efficiency. My longer rides involved getting to R.V. College of
Engineering before 5.20 a.m. at all costs. After that, the traffic picked up
at an alarming pace and the threat of call centre vehicles loomed very
large. These vehicles would whizz past me at ridiculously dangerous
speeds. Besides several near-death experiences trying to avoid reckless
drivers, I had to put up with men trying to out-bike me on their macho
single-speed Hero cycles. But Zippy had gears, and Zippy never lost! I
hurt quite a few egos before sunrise, every single day. If I made it to the
gates of RVCE by 5.20 a.m., I figured I could ride somewhat peacefully
towards Mysore, only having to contend with three-wheelers, two-
wheelers, foot traffic and the odd cow, which I rode past smiling and
mumbling, 'Morning, Kamadhenu!' I imagined its silent response,
*Mmoooo – the weather forecast is muggy today, Mandya bus-stop is
hopping and keep your head up*. Houdini would have been ashamed if he
knew of Kamadhenu's impractical size and equally improbable agility,
materializing out of nowhere on Indian highways and yet staying alive.
I loved those cows. They had compassion, chewed on adversity and
were a permanent prop in my life.

  I typically rode anywhere between three and five hours and on the
way back, I had the option of taking a bus back home in case it got
too late, loading the cycle somewhere on the roof of the bus or in the
back. I defined 'late' as any time after 8.30 a.m., when traffic clogged the
arteries back into the city.

  One day, my greatest fear came true. I had reached RVCE at 5.30
a.m., ten minutes beyond my anointed bike-witching hour. Just as
I thought I had made it and could set off for an hour or two, I felt a

scrape on my right calf and an impact on my handlebar. That is really all I remember. I found myself on the side of the road, caked in mud and blood. I was in shock because I heard no screeching of brakes, no sound of footsteps rushing to my aid, no shadow looming over me, offering a helping hand. I remember looking dazed at what seemed like a Tata Elexi speeding away, the driver throwing a hasty glance over his shoulder. I had to call my mother, which then led to a string of explanations about what the hell I was doing on the road at five in the morning to begin with. But she didn't tell my father or raise an alarm. She quickly called a cab service and sent them to get me. My mother would keep my secret until another series of unfortunate circumstances led to my father discovering my cycling habit.

In the beginning, I ran mostly in the early morning. Then I made the mistake of thinking I could run at Kanteerava Stadium, which was close to Cubbon Park in the centre of Bangalore, later in the day, with no traffic or coaches yelling at me. After my first run at the stadium, I went up to the ladies' room to use the toilet. I found a bunch of half-dressed men using it as a changing room. Rather than looking abashed at being caught in the ladies' restroom, the men looked at me as if I had just landed from the moon. I should have probably expected that because, running on the track that evening, I had been stared at as if I were a UFO – an unidentified female object. I was torn between shock and plain amusement as I made a hasty exit out of there.

A few weeks into my running routine, I discovered that Ulsoor Lake had a rowing team populated by army men. I quickly adapted my routine so that I ran towards the lake and joined the Madras Sappers there in the mornings and some evenings. Being around army men who could run was not the ideal escape from the swim coach I had run into. There were a couple of locals, young men and women from Bangalore, learning how to row. The instructors, especially the lead instructor Frank D'Souza, were very tough on us in the beginning, constantly questioning our discipline as civilians. I began training on the single scull and, in the second week, amateurishly lost my balance and fell into the lake. My saving grace was that I could not stop laughing for a few minutes after I surfaced, thinking that my left butt-cheek must be heavier than my right butt-cheek, which was why the boat capsized. I could not get back in the scull for the life of me and my oars had started to float away rapidly. The next thing I heard was a very loud engine, powered by diesel, and Frank D'Souza at the helm of what looked like a rescue boat. Trying to keep a straight face, I looked at him for instructions. He asked me to hold on and slowly reeled my scull back to shore. I laughed so hard when I got out of the water that the army men realized it was impossible to get me to take myself seriously. It was late in the evening; most of the other intrepid 'students' had left, and we really hit it off. I never felt unsafe running around Ulsoor Lake after that day and did so to my heart's content, until Frank D'Souza left town a few months later.

After that, I quickly got sick of running in traffic, past billboards that seemed to grow in size, advertising heroes that did not live in the neighbourhood, Brazilian footballers and Russian tennis players. I bought myself a treadmill and promptly ended up fighting with my brother over its use. It was hard enough to train in a stuffy room, on a treadmill, without the screaming matches. On particularly bleak days, I reminded myself of a story about an American runner, Frank Shorter, who was pictured running in just shorts, through the deserts of New Mexico. I was not imagining him running as much as recreating the feeling of the sun on my back – there were many weeks when I never stepped out of my office or home, unless it was to buy groceries or supplies. The traffic was unbelievable and sapped any semblance of joy in my life. I even ventured back into Kanteerva, once I was mentally prepared to use the restrooms in the wonderful hotels that dotted the area. Running, I told myself, was the easiest of the three sports to train for in India. I did not need a pool or traffic-free roads, just four months of steady work to afford a treadmill.

My first race towards competing in an Ironman was the Bangalore Half-Marathon, in December 2005. It was the first edition of the Bangalore Marathon, and there were very few women participants. I talked my mother into competing in the senior 3-km walk and we took a bone-rattling auto-rickshaw ride to the start. One's femur, patella, tibia and fibula had more to contend with than just rhyming in the physiotherapist's head, after a rickshaw ride in Bangalore. The start of the senior 3-km walk was an hour later than the start of the half-marathon, so I left my mother sitting in the bleachers, after wishing her luck. Armed with a dubious blue waist-pouch filled with toffees, an oversized cap and conservative clothing, I found myself surrounded by men at the start line. The two women I had seen earlier were lingering at the back and a couple more would appear later. The half-marathon course went from Kanteerva stadium, past the Windsor Manor bridge and back, a little over 21.1 km. Aid stations were simply big tables with some questionable orange liquid, with water arriving much later in the day. The volunteers had no idea what they were doing and it was self-service all the way. Many competitors stopped, sipped water, chattered about the weather and then picked up the pace. I was smiling throughout at the non-seriousness of it all, because it filled my heart to be a part of that event.

Bangalore has a lot of inclines compared to a flatter city like Madras. Running up and down inclines is challenging because they punish the calves and tax the knees and hamstrings. If Arnold Schwarzenegger ever endorsed a complete leg workout, he might have blessed the first Bangalore Half-Marathon course whole-heartedly.

While running, I had psyched myself by repeating, *You are a nimble-footed sitar player. It's okay if no one will marry you because you are so brown and thin, just run to your heart's content.* I was also aiming to place in the top ten, which was delusional at best, considering I had no knowledge of the competition. However, there were only a handful of women competing, out of which an even smaller fraction seemed to be actually running. I overtook two women in the last 3 km and was working pretty hard when I finally entered Kanteerva Stadium. I ran the half-marathon in just about two hours, wearing an oversized t-shirt that billowed in the wind like a sail and felt that I had not really pushed myself. The mark of a good effort is having a rush of lactic acid seize your legs up pretty good, losing a toenail, or both. I felt quite fresh at the end of the race and chided myself for not giving it my best and also for not dressing more appropriately. But I knew it was an honest course, whatever the fashion police may say about my attire.

Close to the finish line, I heard the announcer call out, '... and Ms Vaidyanathan is first, she is looking strong!' I perked up and pushed myself harder and ran faster. Upon finishing I looked around, waiting for cameras, possibly an interview, for TV anchors to come rushing towards me. All I got was a random volunteer trying to spray Iodex on my ankles. The spray was bitingly cold and I yelped, made a face at him and ambled towards the announcer's box to see where my entourage, cameras and garlands were. My heart raced at the prospect of meeting someone influential and important who would recognize that I, the winner, deserved a few perks and amenities to train better.

As it turned out, the announcer had meant my mother, 'Mrs Vaidyanathan', who had finished first in the senior 3-km walk. What the hell had just happened here? I saw my mother grinning sheepishly, caught her eye and both of us laughed till we cried. I had ended up in seventh place in and took home the winnings of Rs 4000. It was the best money I had ever made. Adding to the jubilation was my mother, a cute bundle of silk, carrying her dinner-set prize and grinning from ear to ear. I had just been comprehensively out-dressed and outrun by my mother.

SEPIA

அ-Appa and Amma

அகர முதல எழுத்தெல்லாம் ஆதி
பகவன் முதற்றே உலகு

('A' is the prime of all letters. The Source – God is the prime of
the world.)

It was the first decade after R.S. Venkataraman had declared on All
India Radio, *'Inthiya naadu indru sudandiram petrathu'* (India became
independent today) on 15 August 1947. My mother, Alamelu, was born
in Aathoor, a small village that was an hour's journey from Madurai. My
mother's father, Subramanian Iyer, was a mill-owner without any formal
education. Despite that, he ran seven mills and often fixed complex
mechanical problems based on an intuitive understanding of how things
worked. He even built a machine to make the sieving plates used in rice
mills. He often travelled great distances from Aathoor by foot, to keep
tabs on his business. He also owned a mill in Ayyalur, which was on the
way to Trichy 30 to 40 km away. On the rare occasion that he travelled
by car, it was a classic Ambassador, then called 'Pleasure'. My maternal
grandmother, Mangalam, took great care to manage the family when he
was away. She organized song sessions and had a little room for bhajans
adjacent to their house, opposite the rice mill that my grandfather ran.
She wrote songs too, some of which were later made popular by well-
known artists, without any credit to her. But I think her love for music
far outweighed any desire for external validation.

Entertainment was limited in my grandparents' home to the
radio and listening to the voices of Lotika Ratnam and others, in the

evenings, after the song sessions were over. My mother was one of five sisters and three brothers and the nerdiest of them all. She had read every book in the local library by the age of thirteen and often refused to help with chores, or eat, if she was in the middle of reading a book. My aunt, Sambu, remembers a day when my mother was so engrossed in a book that after many, many warnings, my aunt had to grab her by the hair and drag her out to the courtyard to eat. My mother fought back, kicking and screaming, but my aunt's size and strength got the better of her.

After the ninth grade, one of my mother's teachers spoke to my grandfather about enrolling her in a school in Trichy because Aathoor couldn't do justice to her intelligence, but my grandfather refused. He felt that he did not know how the world worked and he was unwilling to let a girl leave home, even if it was to study. A few years later, shortly before my mother was due to attend college, my grandfather fell ill. This unexpected change in circumstances forced the family to fend for itself and my mother ended up studying in a city college. But the road was paved with heartache and difficulty. They did not have enough money, as her sister was raising a young family at the time. It took grace and fortitude on the part of my aunt Sacchu and uncle Ganesan's to have helped my mother the way they did. Times were hard and she did not even have a proper saree to wear at her graduation – in stark contrast to my own life as a young adult, filled with new clothes and books that arrived as I asked for them.

Mother moved to Calcutta in the 1970s with her older brother Chidambaram and her sister Saroja. She was a gold medallist in chemistry and easily found a job as a patent writer at a leading law firm. Her monthly salary was Rs 350 with 8 per cent PF (Provident Fund). She stayed in a one-bedroom house with her sister, brother-in-law and their five daughters.

My father Vaidyanathan was also one of eight kids and he grew up in a small town called Mannargudi, close to Tanjavur in Tamil Nadu. My paternal grandfather, Sivaraman Iyer, was the headmaster at National High School in Mannargudi and taught English. Growing up, my father was industrious and worked very hard to earn his privileges. His days began at 5 a.m., fetching milk and flowers. There was a small temple at the end of the street on which they lived, *kizh erandaan theru* (lower second street), behind which the milk was sold, and a small water tank, where some people bathed and boys swam. Soon after their morning chores, the children usually got ready for school and had their stationery carefully sorted by their aunt, before they left. Being part of a joint family meant heavy budgeting of family finances. Upon returning home from school, the stationery was checked again, with lost pencils or erasers resulting in a gentle chiding or one less idli for tiffin for repeat offenders.

My grandmother and her sister-in-law ran the household amicably, even in the brief time that they were all together. For the children, entertainment included hours of running around, cycling on a rickety, single-speed bicycle that belonged to Grandpa, and playing till sunset. The occasional movie in Thiruvarur could only be afforded if a relative happened to visit from out of town and my father and his brothers earned some extra annas by carrying luggage to and from the bus-stop, a mile away. Whether they would at all earn that tip was a mystery wrapped in financial conservatism. My father described his heart-rate as remaining very high until the bus with the said relative started up its engine to leave Mannargudi. A gift of four annas would mean a movie ticket, six could include a meal at the local eatery, where my younger uncle had earned a reputation for eating idlis as an accompaniment to sambhar rather than the other way around. Eight annas might even mean an extra treat after the movie.

My father and his friends had voracious appetites for food and adventure. Watching a movie in Thiruvarur meant sneaking out after dark, cycling 18 km one way, then riding back home very late, with almost no lighting, best guided by the moonlight. My grandfather was an academic and an authoritarian with no love for thespians. Upon returning home, my father was inevitably caught and subjected to a sound thrashing. That never stopped him from watching the next movie, however. When he got to college, he had to travel two hours

on a train that ferried milk and flowers to Thanjavur, the closest big
city. My grandmother would wake up at 4 a.m. to pack his breakfast
and lunch and watching her do that, day after day, had a profound
impact on my father. The fate of a young person from rural India is
often defined to a great degree by sheer determination and many, many
hours of hard toil, and my father was determined to make something
of himself. His younger brother was academically brilliant and used to
solve differential equations, using chalk to write on the floor of their
home. My own father still recalls the passage popularly known as 'The
Seven Ages of Man' from Shakespeare's *As You Like It* that he read in
school. And I learned early that people study hard because that is their
only meal-ticket. I was no exception to that rule.

My father's older brother, Raman, was working in Calcutta in
the early fifties. Father moved there to live with him after he turned
seventeen. He worked many odd jobs at first, saved money, and put
himself through a second college to earn a basic degree. In the sixties,
his initial salary was Rs 156 with a dearness allowance of Rs 15. From
this, Rs 13 was deducted towards PF. My father and his brother stayed
in a room at Ballygunge in south Calcutta. They shared a bathroom
and four toilets with twenty other young men from different parts of
the country. Getting into those toilets early in the morning was like
a scramble for gold starring Blondie, Tuco and Angel Eyes. My father
and his friends ate at a small hotel adjacent to the rooms, where they
prepaid the owner Rs 30 for 60 or 62 meals a month, depending on the
month. Money went much further in those days.

My parents met in Calcutta. My uncle Chidambaram first met my
father at the local eatery and struck up a friendship. Since my mother
had a steady job and my father was still struggling at the time, she
often ended up paying for their dates, which involved long tram rides
through Calcutta, gazing lovingly at all the cakes at Flury's they could
not afford, and weekend shopping for handbags, which ultimately my
mother paid for herself. In my father's defence, when it came to the
touchy subject of dowry, which was a norm back in the day, he paid it
himself on my mother's behalf without telling anyone.

Later in life too, my father would support my mother's career immensely, and keep her away from the cacophony of his family and, when required, hers.

After Calcutta, my parents lived in New Delhi for several years. They had a small place in Malviya Nagar and I was born there. My mother was rising through the ranks as a patent draftsman, having become the second woman patent agent to qualify in India, but she still had trouble convincing her peers that she needed to be dropped off first by the company car so she could pick me up early from day-care. After a few months, Mangalam-paati came to take care of me and, with my father's schedule being more accommodating, my mother could meet the demands of a job that required her to work over twelve hours a day.

My brother was born in Ayyampetai, where we lived when I was a few years old. My aunt Sambu took care of us when we were very young and I remember lazy days spent swimming in the Kudamurutti river, near Ayymapetai. I also remember the day my brother was born – there was a lot of activity in the house. He was much quieter than I was as a child and often, according to my mother anyway, I could understand him better than most. If he wanted something – advice, chocolates, anything – I was his go-to girl. It was a very special title for me. My brother and I being two and a half years apart put even more pressure on my mother's career and she decided to quit her job. My parents moved to Bangalore in the eighties, two kids in tow, a stone's throw away from extended family. They decided to carve out a niche of their own and started a small business.

Our grandfathers passed away early but our grandmothers would visit us at frequent intervals. My father's mother, Parvatham-paati, came more often than my mother's, for whom it was a much longer journey, since she lived with my uncle Chidambaram in Calcutta. I remember my father's mother as a very disciplined person who was also extremely devout. She would wake up early, until she was very old, and take a bath. No one was allowed to touch her till she finished preparing the morning meal. Stupid and somewhat spoiled children that we were, it was a big joke for us to touch paati before she prepared that meal. My father let our misbehaviour slip once, twice with a warning, but the third time, he really gave it to us with a tight slap and clear and loud instructions to stop being jerks. When I look back, I can see that my parents resembled none of their siblings or relatives, but they respected their way of life and they required us to do the same.

In Bangalore, we lived in an odd-shaped house, with one bedroom and a small second room in front, attached via a bathroom to the rest of the house. This room was used as the office in which my parents started their business. On weekdays, we were in school by early morning and home by late afternoon. On days when we did not have homework, I remember helping my parents stick stamps on their outgoing mail or pretending to read my mother's neatly written drafts. Although my brother and I fought quite a lot, as children do, and drove our mother nuts, we loved her company. She made a huge effort to take care of us, cook us many wonderful meals and constantly encouraged us to be ourselves. She was herself extremely busy, but every spare moment she had was spent trying to make our lives better. Many nights, I would hear my parents in their office, talking or typing furiously on their Godrej typewriter, preparing drafts, while I sat quietly in the adjacent bathroom just to hear the sound of their voices. To this day, as different as my parents are, my father being the life of any party and my mother a quiet observer with a sharp wit, they complement each other in life and love, and in their ability to face any challenge the world throws at them.

Thespians and Thayirsaadam

Ootla solityu vantiyaa?

(Did you tell your folks that you won't be coming back home?)
—Rickshaw driver, Chennai

As a child, I attended a convent for my early schooling in Bangalore, until 1995. I joined the rest of my classmates in wearing some frock-type uniform with a light blue shirt and a dark blue skirt. The uniforms created the same kind of visual chorus we were shooting for during our prayers in assembly, with '*Our Father in Heaven*' being recited at a frantic pitch. I wore glasses to correct myopia, with lenses so thick that when focused just right, they could set ants on fire. I also passionately avoided physical training (PT), which involved marching in the strangest formations all over the school grounds, proving occasionally that Brownian motion is not the only abstract, stochastic, continuous time-process. We never felt physically exhausted, just bored. I made up every excuse possible to sit out of marching class. Mrs Jeemol, our sports teacher, would exasperatedly exclaim, 'Child, moving is not a crime.' I would smile weakly, point at my stomach and pretend to be under the spell of a rare tropical disease for the first five minutes, after which I would get back to my books. I think now that Jeemol probably saw right through the super-nerd in me.

I was never first in class, never first at anything except English, history and geometry. During PT, my main aim was to get brighter at all the things I was not so bright at, so that I could improve my ranking

from third or fifth to first. But yes, I did cycle to school, nearly 7 km
one way.

Cluny Convent High School required of its students everything a
'good' school at the time was supposed to. We were punished for being
late, we were proud to finish assignments early or right on time, we
loved showing off to some of our kinder teachers, and we could speak
plainly to our headmistress. Most of my classmates loved school as
much as I did. Whatever they were good at was encouraged in one
class or another. We had authoritarian teachers, we had goofy teachers
and we had incredibly scholarly teachers, such as my computer science
teacher who made me feel that writing code in BASIC was the grandest
occupation a girl could have. Bangalore was always up to date with
technology and we were starting to hear about a company called Yahoo!,
which fuelled the passionate interest I had developed in programming.

Every evening, I had two to three hours of hide-and-seek, climbing
trees and running around to look forward to. A group of kids in my
neighbourhood, boys and girls of all shapes and sizes, played together
till sunset and sometimes, late into the night. Our streets were empty
of traffic, except for fathers returning from work on their scooters or
supply-men ferrying things to our homes. Our playground was spread
over several blocks of houses, which made playing hide-and-seek a lot
of fun. We also climbed a lot of trees, most often the infamous ucche
kai tree, with its bladder-shaped flower-buds, out of which we would
squirt water mercilessly at anybody who did not climb up fast enough.
I remember my playmates were equally competitive, irrespective of
gender. Especially while climbing those trees.

Nintendo ruled the roost after 9 p.m. We were no strangers to
Mario, Luigi, Princess Peach and Toad. Well past 9 p.m., after several
hours of play and very little homework, we would watch a few minutes
of *The Bold and The Beautiful* on Star TV, another luxury we grew up
with. I could never remember who was bold and who was beautiful,
but I had a mad crush on Ronn Moss, whom I only knew then as Ridge
Forrester. If he was on a TV screen, I was watching that screen. My
mother had invested in a dial-up internet connection, which was my

ticket to the rest of the world. Internet Relay Chat (IRC) was big back then; we had pen-pals on email, met many of them during the year and tried to be as fashionable as the people we met. One memory I have is of an IRC meet-up at a pizza joint near Kanteerva Stadium. Having never eaten a pizza before in my life and not wanting to look silly, I studiously picked up a fork and knife and attacked the massive pie in front of me. I noticed everyone else was eating with their hands and in my hurry to set down my cutlery, sent a piece of pizza flying from the first floor of the restaurant to the ground floor. I made some friends for life after that outing.

Soon after finishing my tenth standard board exams and spending all of those ten years at Cluny Convent in Bangalore, I decided I had to go to Madras to study for my eleventh and twelfth. I wanted to prepare for the Indian Institute of Technology Joint Entrance Exams (IIT-JEE), by taking extra classes. But after just two weeks of boarding school, I jumped the fence, found a payphone and frantically asked my father to get me out of there. The school's administration seemed to be lacking, I told him, as none of the facilities that had been advertised actually existed. The classes were terrible and I felt I was getting dumber by the second. My parents were perplexed. I had insisted on going to Madras. I had insisted on being in a boarding school. Finding another school two weeks into the academic term was almost unheard of. Madras took education very seriously.

I ended up finally at a new, very conservative and highly academic school at Mylapore which was in some ways even worse than the one I had fled. In any case, I had my freedom at home, which was a small one-bedroom flat belonging to my periamma and periappa (maternal aunt and uncle), who were away on a three-year pilgrimage. They were kind enough to rent my family the little flat in T-Nagar, which was literally the greatest olfactory treat of any neighbourhood in Madras. I had no complaints living in that flat though; it brought out the best in me. I had an overbearing neighbour, who spoke to me exclusively in Telugu. Once I entered the gates of the apartment complex, I would hear her voice from a distance –

'Bhagunnara Anu?'

'Yes, Aunty, I am fine.'

'Meeru emu chestunaaru.'

'Nothing Aunty, I have to go to IIT tuitions now.'

'Bhojanam chesava.'

'Yes Aunty, the Golkonda, sorry, the gongura was great with thayirsaadam.'

'Tuition tarvaata miru *Dilwale Dulhaniya* film chudalakune?'

'I don't have time, Aunty.'

I could never understand a word of what she said, but she insisted on feeding the 'poor thin girl from Bangalore' on a daily basis. By no stretch of the imagination was I thin then. But I was living alone, which was unheard of for a sixteen-year-old to do, and so this neighbour of mine made sure I was well-fed and safe. She embodied the sort of maternal kindness that is so underrated today. She was a neighbour, not a relative or a friend. She was nosy. She did check on me more often than she needed to. However, she never pried beyond a point and she never made me feel uncomfortable. I was glad that someone was watching out for me in the absence of my parents and my brother, whom I missed deeply, every day.

My mom knew I was struggling, for she was constantly in the loop on my misadventures.

Getting into trouble and confessing to her, then extracting a million promises from her that she would not tell my father, was nothing new or unusual. She knew that moving to a conservative school in Madras after spending most of my childhood in Bangalore had come as a complete shock to me. To add to my woes, I had recently cut off all my hair and was 'that Iyer girl with short hair'! From the first day, I was isolated. None of the kids were friendly. They had all formed their little cliques and would not budge out of them. For the first four months, I took the bus from home in T. Nagar to school in Mylapore. I was made fun of for my short hair even on the bus, with the smart-alec conductor asking me the same snarky question every evening. 'Paiyana ponna?' (Is this a boy or a girl?) Then he would pose the question loudly to the rest of the

bus and they would respond with a resounding chorus of 'Ponnu saar!'
(It's a girl!) I used to laugh out loud each time because truly, this was
the only light-hearted part of my day, given the unfriendly company
in school. At the end of a difficult, ridicule-ridden four months, my
mother, without my father's permission, decided to buy me a moped.
After managing to get to school in one piece on the first day, I forgot
how to start it in the evening. Rachana, the brightest girl in the class,
who for the first few months had thought my parents were divorced
and that I was a runaway from home, given that I lived alone, came up
to me and showed me how to open the petrol gauge. The twenty-five
minutes spent trying to start that blasted moped under the glare of all
the girls in that girls' school were the longest twenty-five minutes of
my life. But the moped and I soon became great friends and went to a
lot of places together. I was grateful to my mother for buying it for me,
for cultivating my independence. She was my confidante then and she
remains my confidante to this day.

Madras was incredibly tough on my gregarious outlook. Extra-
curricular activities were not encouraged at my new school. Anyone
who did not *only study* became a pet peeve with the teachers. Suddenly,
my psyche did a 180-degree turn and sport seemed like a promised land.
I took to doing all the drills on the minimal school grounds. The flip side
of the heavy focus on academics in Madras was the vibrant scene with
cultural festivals in schools. I started taking part in speech competitions
and participated in several debates at various inter-school events and
made every excuse possible to stay out of the confines of DAV Senior
Secondary. At one such event, my classmate and I decided that we
would take up singing. There was a rule that a school had to participate
in a minimum number of events to be ranked. I had participated in
the speech, debate and essay writing, and singing seemed easier to do
than, say, dancing. When I imagined myself dancing at these cultural
competitions, I pictured myself atop a billboard, much like Prabhudeva,
the Indian version of Michael Jackson on two feet, but his dance moves
from the movie *Kadhalan* were the benchmark that year and I didn't
think it was wise to try and match them.

Unfortunately, the song I wanted to sing required a drummer. I will never forget what happened next. I got on stage, gung-ho about placing or even winning, as I had clobbered the competition in the other three events, and confidently belted out a tune. We had to sing for three whole minutes to be considered song-worthy, but halfway through, I had a sneaking suspicion that everyone in the audience was snickering. Finally, at around two minutes I realized that I had not heard a single drum beat. I turned around and saw my friend, bless her heart, frozen with stage fear, a drumstick in her raised hand, mouth agape. When I turned slowly to face the audience, they started roaring. I fought to keep a straight face but once we got off stage, in typical Madras fashion, we heard someone comment, 'Paapa yenna drums vasikidu pa!' (Superb drumming by this babe!) and burst out laughing. Our friendship was short-lived though, because back in school on Monday, she was reminded that I was not part of any group and I went back to being treated like the plague.

At the end of my eleventh standard, I was confronted with bigger problems. The evening classes for the IIT-JEE were held in a government school in a low-lying area in Mylapore and once the monsoon started, the place suffered severe waterlogging. There were three professors teaching math, physics and chemistry to prepare more than 400 students for the exams. The physics teacher, Professor Badrinarayanan, was the grand conductor of the orchestra. Every day he would stand on the balcony, yelling at us and taunting the weaker ones to walk faster. His classes and tactics were legendary. He had students from all parts of the country, studying for the third or even the fourth time to pass the JEE. There was a huge population of students from Kota, Rajasthan, and the state of Andhra Pradesh. Every group seemed to have a nickname; folks from Andhra were called goltis, we Tamilians were called thayirsaadams, folks from Kerala were called mallus and anyone outside Tamil Nadu, Andhra, Kerala and Karnataka were called Narth Indians. Later in life, I would understand this syndrome of group-creation as fairly universal.

I found camaraderie with a girl named Krithiga, who was from

Bombay and who, like me, wanted to qualify for the IITs. She too was a misfit in the conservative world of double standards we found ourselves in, struggling to deal with the treatment meted out to us foreign Tamilians by the resident Tamilians. For a long time, we both wondered why the professors made us come to this school with terrible facilities. I now believe that they just wanted to weed out the weakest among us. During the first monsoon, we would wade through hip-high water with our book bags held above our heads. After three months, I fell very ill. I was worried about what would happen, as they were strict about attendance. School attendance, tuition attendance and keeping my sanity seemed to have me walking on eggshells with my classmates or earning the scorn of my teachers. I could never get anything right. It seemed like failure was an option at every step. My mother made an emergency visit to Madras to admit me to the local hospital when my fever would not break after three days. My very quiet younger brother had started to pray for me, as my family felt sure something very bad was about to happen. I had contracted a rare disease, leptospirosis, the occurrence of which is closely related to exposure to stagnant water. If undiagnosed, it would have led to kidney and liver failure. I could have died. Luckily for me, they diagnosed it with hours left to spare.

As luck would have it, the IIT-JEE exam was cancelled in 1997 and a re-examination was announced. As the papers screamed 'IIT Papers Leaked in Lucknow', I could not laugh for once – two years of my life had vanished. Since a few of us had placed all our bets on getting through the IIT-JEE, we had not focused enough on the board exams, which could gain us entrance into engineering programmes at local colleges in the state. A lot of the girls who attended tuitions dropped out in the twelfth standard to concentrate on the boards instead of losing focus with the JEE, which required a totally different effort. Krithiga and I stuck to our guns and failed gloriously. I moved back to Bangalore to regroup and figure out what to do. My dream of studying computer engineering seemed distant, let alone at an IIT. I did start an engineering programme, paying a fat fee to study a branch of engineering I was not interested in. I suppose, in my family, our brains are not wired to accept the obvious. I pretty much lazed around until February, then took the Scholastic Aptitude Tests (SATs) on a lark. Succeeding on merit was important to me and if that was not to be in India, I was eager to look for other options. The SATs were fairly easy given what we had been preparing for, and I ended up getting a full scholarship to Knox College, a liberal arts college in Galesburg, Illinois, to study computer science.

'merica

'Sal, we gotta go and never stop going till we get there.'
'Where we going, man?'
'I don't know but we gotta go.'

—*On the Road*, Jack Kerouac

My father decided to accompany me to Galesburg, which was a couple of hours' drive from Chicago. When we landed at O'Hare in early 1998, with two big suitcases, two little suitcases and my backpack, an admissions counsellor greeted us. He drove us to Galesburg and explained everything along the way. The first night in the hotel was a strange one; the first sounds we heard were the wails of police sirens. We did not sleep much that night, but a few days later, my father and I attended orientation and he returned to Bangalore in the same week. He appeared calm as we said our goodbyes, but I knew he was as terrified as I was. I did not cry until he left, but once his bus to O'Hare was out of sight, I ran to my room and burst into tears.

Once the semester kicked off at Knox College, I realized that the engineering programme they had promised with the University of Illinois at Urbana Champaign (UIUC), which is what made me accept the scholarship, was overrun by local admits rather than international students. UIUC was a state-funded college and had to pick from the local pool first. Being very competitive and an excellent engineering college, there was no dearth of potential candidates. It was like the IIT-JEE all over again. This time though, I was less concerned. At the end of the academic session at Knox, I got on a bus on my own and headed off to Chicago.

I enrolled in summer school at the University of Illinois in Chicago, found a sub-lease online with an Indian graduate student called Latha, who lived within a stone's throw of downtown Chicago, and quickly became my adopted mother.

The Chicago Bulls beat the Utah Jazz at the NBA finals that summer and the whole city went nuts. Michael Jordan, who was the most valued player that year, owned a restaurant on LaSalle Street, which was close to where we lived. The night of the Bulls' victory was pretty noisy. The air was electric and we did not need a television to know what had just happened.

It was a splendid summer. I took a creative writing class, a physics class and a chemistry class. I met Latha's friend, Krishna, who was pursuing a PhD at Purdue University and resembled an elongated, six-foot version of Asterix with his huge moustache and curly dark hair. He had gone sweet on Latha, who was having none of it. In order to impress her, Krishna was very nice to me and I took him up on his offer to hitch a ride to Purdue, to enquire about their undergraduate programme in computer engineering. Purdue was a private college in a different state, Indiana, whose alumni included Neil Armstrong. I figured, if this college was good enough for him, it would be good enough for me.

The first admissions counsellor I met at Purdue was south Indian. The minute I spotted her with her saree and nose-ring, I caught myself desperately trying to please her in the hope that she would invite me home for some delicious dosas and filter coffee. My hopes were dashed as soon as she opened her mouth. She was discouraging, to say the least. 'You are too late...', 'You will never be admitted...', 'You will never find accommodation...', etc. At some point in that first conversation, I started counting backwards from 1000 to drown out her voice. I asked her just one question: 'What will I need to do to get past the first year? Because I don't want to waste time'. She said I would have to clear all the tests that the college had for students who wanted credit for first-year courses in the engineering programme, the first-year courses being common to all branches, but not before letting me know, yet again, that 'You will not be able to.'

I then met another counsellor at the International Students Office who said I would definitely be admitted, just not guaranteed housing. Armed with this new information, I decided to take the tests. I asked Krishna, whom I had hitched a ride with, if I could sleep on his sofa for the week, which he happily agreed to. I passed all the tests, got my admission sorted, and went back to Chicago to finish the term. Within a month, I was back on a bus to Galesburg, where I packed all my belongings into one big suitcase and one big trash bag with dirty clothes from the trip. I couldn't be bothered to do laundry. A whole new computer lab with SUN machines, poetry for my geeky soul, was waiting for me at Purdue.

At Purdue, the second counsellor put me with a group of students to help me integrate. The majority of them, I discovered, were the first in their family to attend college. Not surprisingly, most were African-American or Hispanic. The one thing we all had in common was that we were on our own. Moving away from Knox College meant I was without a scholarship and suddenly there was huge financial pressure to deal with. This was not something my family had bargained for, but my parents supported my decision anyway. All of us in that group worked part-time at some job or the other, in addition to classes. Without a proper support system to make peace with the incredible disparities in Purdue's student wealth, we only had each other to bank on. Three of my friends from that group, Eddie, Frank and Rees, got me through the first semester with a lot of laughs, despite the heartache. Eddie signed up with the Reserve Officers Training Corps (ROTC), the hiring ground for the US Armed Forces within colleges and also delivered pizza, which did not help my waistline one bit. Frank worked in mail delivery and, on campus, at a fraternity. Rees temped off-campus but never missed a single group meeting. He was the quietest of them and deeply vulnerable, but without any trace of self-pity. He once told me that the group meeting every week was a shot of adrenaline that got him through the long work hours. All four of us worked twenty hours a week that semester and I had a 30-credit workload, which was well above average. I did the math and understood that the quicker I graduated, the less my father would have to spend on fees. My parents never told me to work, but I knew that the costs were not easy to cover. I wanted to learn how to manage time, as my American peers were doing with extra jobs. If they could work and attend classes, I was certainly not going to throw myself a pity party or ring home for money.

There were a handful of Indians among my classmates at Purdue, to whom I was never properly introduced because living off-campus, although cheaper, meant no interaction in the college mess or at other social events. I was too shy and too busy to strike up a lasting conversation in any case. I could not afford the social outings or identify with their obsession with the latest sitcom at the time, *Friends*. One group had mapped each character from the sitcom onto themselves and played out dialogues in real-time. Television, affectionately called the Boob Tube in 'merica, seemed like a global epidemic. When I did brave an episode of *Friends*, I laughed hard but promptly forgot to watch the following episodes. Living off-campus and working a job was no fairy tale – it turned out that I did not have time for television.

The fall I started at Purdue, I moved in with Indian graduate students in a largely Indian neighbourhood. Because I was younger and pretty talkative in that group, I quickly became the butt of all their jokes. I took it sportingly enough, along with some other charming qualities they had – discussing ragas and the more pedantic aspects of the Vedas. Then, one day, I came home to find the milk bottles marked with permanent markers – to ration groceries, I was told. We all pooled towards food supplies, so I could not understand this at all. For my mother, who had come visiting after my first year in the US, it was the last straw. She would not hear of my staying on with my older roommates. I tried to reason with her that I did not mind, saying, 'Amma, it's okay, I'll try to get along. This is close to college. Didn't you always say we should all try to get along?' She looked at me, a little exasperated, having to rephrase what she had always said to me about being kind to people and said, 'Yes, you do need to get along with people, as long as they are fair and kind to you. Living here seems to be more stress than fun.' She picked up a newspaper, scouted for places, took the help of a different set of students and moved me into a studio apartment as quickly as she could. To her, my mind space was precious, no matter my grades or social outings.

The studio I ended up living in was on the other side of campus, with another set of apartments up the road, where I would eventually meet my best friends in college – a band of itinerant Indian graduate students from IIT Madras. No matter how many years pass between meetings, or how many milestones we cross, we always seem to be able to pick up just where we left off, as if it were yesterday. Sanjeev Paklapatti, fondly called Pat (pronounced 'putt') was studying for a PhD in aeronautical engineering at Purdue. He was a serious squash player and marathoner, and it was he who introduced me to running. When he was not solving equations in his head, he was helping me finish my Signals and Systems homework. He taught me discrete mathematics with as much aplomb as he introduced me to a 3-km loop that went around campus. He convinced me that I would not die of an aneurysm if I ran that loop. At that time, I thought aerobics was the worst thing a woman could do to lose weight, but I couldn't even vaguely imagine running.

Most evenings after classes, I would ramble into the house Pat shared with three other boys, also among my best friends till date, to find him sprawled on the floor while Tony, who was studying for a PhD in mathematics, lay stretched out on the couch, scribbling on yellow notepads. From the kitchen rose the smell of something divine being cooked, and old black-and-white movie music played in the background. There was never any talk of grocery bills, milk consumption or ragas. Everyone contributed the best they could and conversation flowed across so many interesting topics. While I understood very little, I was fascinated by Tony, Pat, Manish and Sunil's commitment to their PhD work. They truly loved what they did and they were rarely snobbish about it. They tried their best to keep me, a lowly undergraduate, in their conversation. They worked incredible hours and their social lives seemed to be restricted to that living room. Sunil, in particular, would keep locking himself out of his lab, or home, or both, and end up coming over to get spare keys, which he wisely left at Pat's place.

Although Manish would wisecrack with everyone else, he watched out for me like a protective elder brother. This was the time when the idea of getting a PhD was first sown in my head. I thought that if I could love something as much as that, it would be a smashing hit.

By the second year, I did find a good group of friends among my classmates. I had been acutely aware of being one in five women in a graduating class of a hundred and fifty in computer engineering. I forced myself not to make too much of that statistic except that it meant that I took no shit from my male peers. We women stuck together as much as we could and never apologized for our love for science. Laurie (who was from Indiana), Chyou Hseih (from Hong Kong) and I were a three-girl band that stayed together over my three years at Purdue.

We tried to make friends with as many of our male classmates as we could tolerate, minus the letches, the moochers, the condescending a-holes and of course, the peacocks. Many of our classmates thought of private college as something they were entitled to, and we found that hilarious. The rate of burn-out was very high and having a bad attitude about the hardship was a mood-kill. Since we constantly found ourselves in the company of men, the standing joke at parties with fellow engineers was that we were always going around saying, 'We are gay men' in a desperate attempt to find boyfriends. The time between homework, projects and classes was spent checking out the beautiful, well-dressed women in liberal arts, with a few male specimens from engineering. I was in awe of how flawless, rested and calm these women looked – *as if they were enjoying life.* I wished I could make friends with them, but Laurie constantly reminded me that we were 'one of the guys'.

After graduating from Purdue in three years with an insane course load, I drove down to Raleigh, North Carolina, to get a master's degree in October 2001. By then, I had ended up sitting in on a lot of graduate classes and learned as much as I could about computer architecture – building microprocessors was a thrilling prospect. I was obsessed with my research. During the week, I would be at work by 8 a.m. after a morning run, and stayed there until the late hours of the night.

While North Carolina was a part of the Bible belt, there was an active student population that was very liberal. On my first day at NC State, I was looking for the administration building to register for classes when I saw this tall girl with green hair, who seemed very relaxed and, even better, seemed to know where she was going. I asked her where the building was and she very kindly gave me directions. We struck up a conversation while crossing the street. Wanting desperately to impress her, because she exuded this warmth that I was immediately drawn to, I tried a pop-culture TV reference by pointing at a brightly painted building and blurting out, 'That is so gay!' She looked blank and I was confused: Did she not watch *Friends?* Turned out, she did not watch TV, so suddenly I was even more desperate to be friends with her. She told me her name was Aurora, and she would become a mainstay in my life very soon. She invited me to a party at her house that weekend, and when I got there, I found the door open – which, as I would discover over time, was the way it always was. I also met several people who would go on to become my friends. Her roommates had dreadlocks, a vegetable garden, they recycled, held respectable day jobs, and a few were Christians. They explained the nuances of religion as they saw it, minus the dogma, and introduced me to Janis Joplin and Fleetwood Mac. One of their visitors said, 'I have finally met a bunch of people who live out their stereotypes.' I learned a lot about the politics of food that year, how blind consumption and shopping are not everything, how much recycling helps and how it is possible for a set of old friends under one roof and varied paths through life to share their experiences with one another so that everyone learns something in the process.

Aurora introduced me to what I perceived as a more *real* version of America, which did not involve retail therapy, incessant talk of sitcoms or sleeping beyond 8 a.m. When I met her, she was working summers to pay for her tuition and helped out as much as she could within the community. She loved books, dreamed of travelling when she could afford it, and was incredibly independent. The subterranean culture of America she espoused demonstrated a very well-defined backbone and an individualism that was refreshing to me. Purdue had a different crowd of people compared to NC State, which was exactly that: state-funded, and therefore a lot more diverse and humble. In getting to know Aurora, I also got to know 'merica a bit better.

On my bus ride from Galesburg to West Lafayette before starting my term at Purdue three years earlier, I'd had a copy of Jack Kerouac's *On the Road* clutched in my hand, picked up at a thrift store. I had bought the book purely for the title, considering I was about to embark on a 200+ mile journey on my own at the age of eighteen, after uprooting myself from the last home my father had accompanied me to. I had fallen in love then, with the Beat Poets, a group of writers in America who rose to prominence after World War II. However, it was not until I met Aurora that I understood that, like India, 'merica had several sub-cultures and several experiences to offer.

In Raleigh, I was enjoying living alone, learning to cook and packing my day effectively with activities. I lived close to my lab, ran religiously, and made it a point to enjoy my weekends. After coming across an ad asking for volunteers, I picked up work for a few hours for Raleigh Rescue, which was a homeless shelter. My single task was reading to the children there, who had faced several upheavals in their lives. Their favourite story, I soon discovered, was *The Very Quiet Cricket*. When I started working at Raleigh Rescue, I was not sure whether I would like it. To be honest, I was a little afraid. But my fears were completely unfounded. Once I got there, I felt perfectly at home. More than I did in many other places, actually.

Every week, I would take one full day off from cooking to eat the awful food at the student cafeteria. I went there not so much for the food as to meet Mrs Rogers, the cashier. She was a tough woman who always had a smile, a kind word and the right change. One of my part-time jobs during my undergraduate years was dishwashing. Once I told her that, she always waved, smiled, asked how my classes were going and told me to hang in there when we had some long nights finishing assignments. My classmate and friend Ann was my partner in crime during these visits as she lived on campus and always ate at the cafeteria. I remember Ann as being very determined, with a great attitude and a healthy respect for life and its opportunities. That really rubbed off on me.

A few weeks after arriving in Raleigh, I stopped at a local pizzeria, which served up pizza slices for a dollar, to grab a bite. I was standing in line when the television caught my eye. The World Trade Center in New York had been bombed. I did not know what the World Trade Center signified at the time but my jaw dropped, as did everyone else's. We stood in line without paying for nearly ten minutes, transfixed. What followed was utter frenzy. I called all my friends at Purdue, just to be sure no one had been travelling at the time. One of my Indian friends was headed towards New York and I could not reach him. In a state of panic, I called his mother in Bangalore. She had not heard the news and I felt like a complete jerk for having disturbed her. This was only the beginning though, for he would be in radio silence for nearly two days and in that time, his mother reached out to me frequently to see whether I had spoken to him.

A few months later, my old friend Laurie, whose family had once invited me to their home in Indiana for Christmas, sent me a disturbing email, which said things like, 'You foreigners want to take over the United States, but always know that I know where you live.' I was in a state of shock reading that email. I thought I knew her very well. I had spent several hours with her on class projects and long weekends. I had not been a foreigner then. On a bus ride not long after, I was to encounter a slightly drunk man speaking in a heavy Southern accent, who said, 'You f-ing Pakis, why don't you get out of here?' When I told Aurora and Ann about these exchanges, they hugged me and told me to forget about these incidents immediately. I listened to them.

In Raleigh, I started to appreciate how much stronger one feels when surrounded by peers with similar quandaries, fears, hopes and dreams. North Carolina was a revelation in its own right. I met some wonderful people, learned a lot about counter-culture and working-class America and started to see myself in a different light.

All through this time, I ran regularly, in and around Walnut Creek on my shorter runs, and Lake Raleigh and Lake Johnson on the longer ones. When I wanted to spend more than three hours by myself, I would go to Umstead State Park.

This park embraced the cities of Raleigh, Cary and Durham and was a treasure trove of trees, birds, little animals and many trails. I often found myself on the Reedy Creek trail, taking a couple of detours into other trails every now and then. There were plenty of birds in the forest. Owls, kingfishers and woodpeckers were the ones I saw most often. Thrushes, chickadees, nuthatches and bluebirds sang to me whenever I stopped to listen. Being in the forest helped me stay calm and re-focus on the simple act of running. I also found it easier to talk to the trees and the birds than to most human beings, even those I loved. The trees did not judge, forewarn or worry about the weather. They just stood there, breathing magic air into my lungs, asking for nothing back from me. Once the winter arrived, it brought with it buffleheads – small ducks. Later in the spring, closer to April, there was an abundance of wildflowers with quaint names such as spring beauty and azure bluet. Alongside hardwoods including oak and beech were flowering trees, the eastern rosebud with its pink flowers and many rhododendrons. The forest made me consider the seasonality of everything. The birds did not need visas to migrate; they just went where they pleased. Running down a corridor of trees, I wondered if they thought I was a foreigner too. But if I heard them right, they replied, *You are fire, water and air, we are no different, who is foreign where?* Encouraged by this, I asked them if they thought I was an *f-ing Paki.* The trees sportingly cleared that up for me, silently whispering, *Just shut up and run.* I would have many such conversations, discussing matters of the heart, head and lungs with my unmoving tree-druids cloaked in blue, brown and green.

I stayed only a year at Raleigh because I found my master's programme very slow. After Purdue, where I had a huge course load and a part-time job, a university where graduate students took only three classes a semester did not offer enough of a challenge. I doubled up on my classes and decided to graduate in a year. Five months away from the end of the year, I was accepted to the PhD programme in electrical engineering at the University of Wisconsin at Madison.

In 2002, before summer kicked in, I packed up a majority of my stuff, intending to transfer it to a storage unit in Madison. I would have no time to move after I finished my summer classes, so with the help of a friend in Raleigh, I made the seventeen-hour journey to Madison, with the UHaul, covering close to a thousand miles over the Easter break. The road trip was a bit of a disaster as it turned out my friend wanted to marry me and he popped the question somewhere between Virgina and Greensboro. At first, I thought I had heard wrong. He was a tall, good-looking boy, one of my most trusted colleagues and friends at Raleigh, honest and fun to hang out with. I asked him to pull over at a gas station, pretending to need to use the bathroom. The song that was playing at the gas station was 'Two less lonely people in the world' by Air Supply. I laughed my head off in the bathroom, looked at myself in the mirror and then laughed some more. I loved this guy as a friend but simply could not fathom getting married at twenty-one.

After the insufferable slowness of summer school and long days writing my thesis, the last two weeks in Raleigh started on a countdown. I was writing the acknowledgements for my master's thesis, spell checking and repeating my experiments to verify the graphs. Sometime around midnight on Monday, I noticed inconsistencies in my research results on the verification run. At first, I thought I was just sleepy and headed home to get a good night's rest. The next morning, however, it became evident that my results from simulations were erroneous. In my last set of graphs, I found inconsistencies I could not explain. I spent all week trying to figure it out, but had no luck. My thesis presentation was only days away and I was torn. Somewhere in my head I knew that no one was going to verify those graphs and I could always make up some excuse for only 4–5 graphs being wrong or inconsistent. But I also knew that if I took the easy way out, pursuing a PhD after my master's degree would become less meaningful, even to me. With three days to go, I decided that if I could not find out what was wrong, I would tell my thesis advisor the same evening and postpone my presentation. This had a lot of implications including a potential delay in starting my PhD. I was stressed beyond belief, had not slept in days and could not figure out what was wrong. By noon, things looked hopeless. I emailed my advisor, set up a meeting for 4 p.m. and went for a run. I showered and was back in the office by 2 p.m., thinking, 'What the hell, I'll try one last thing. It sure as hell would be funny if it's a stack overflow bug, which is what my thesis is all about.'

Guess what? The stack overflow bug that I had not even considered turned out to be the cause of the problem, leading the simulator to cough up weird numbers. I did meet my advisor at 4 p.m., and proudly reported that all my verifications were finally done. Aurora was also graduating with me, albeit with a bachelor's degree, and we had a going-away party, with the theme being Mohawks and Dupattas. It was quite a hit, with half the population in mock (and some real) Mohawks and the other half sporting most of my wardrobe from Bangalore. It was a phenomenal night. When one drunken reveller asked me 'Anu, are you lesbian?', I replied, 'Not yet.' Three days later, Aurora and I got on a plane to Alaska for a week-long tramp, which was our graduation gift to ourselves.

Belonging

Guys like us, that work on ranches, are the loneliest guys in the world.
They got no family. They don't belong no place…
With us it ain't like that. We got a future.

—*Of Mice and Men*, John Steinbeck

Madison was a mixed bag of tricks. In the first fortnight of September 2002, I was very excited to be there. I lived opposite the lab I worked in and, looking at the sign of 'Orchard Street' outside my apartment window, I pinched myself every day, to make sure I was not dreaming. I was even more excited to discover the local arboretum, a little piece of heaven replete with spruces, pines, firs, oaks and the funny-to-me Indian grass.

The university was very liberal in its stated outlook and drew some of the brightest minds across departments. In my first semester there, I was enrolled in graduate school in engineering and worked as a researcher in computer sciences. I was paid a stipend for the research but then, my advisor decided to move at the end of the semester. Before I could ponder over my next move, or figure out a different research group to work for, sometime in December, I got a phone call.

A voice on the other end said, 'Hey, this is Ron. Am I speaking to Anu?'

I frowned, trying to remember if I had paid my last credit-card bill. I thought I had. Cautiously, I replied, 'Yes, this is Anu.'

The voice continued, 'Hey, I am calling from IBM, we wanted to see if you are interested in an internship at Extreme Blue in Austin with our hypervisor team.' I was furious. I was sure this was Andy pulling my leg. Working on building a hypervisor, which can be understood as a thin sheet of code between hardware and software, alongside some of the best researchers in the industry, was all I could talk about at every group meeting.

I said, 'Screw you, Andy!' and hung up.

A few minutes later, the phone rang again. Turned out it really was someone called Ron, and he really was from IBM. I was sure they had got my name wrong. Convinced that this Ron was polysyllabically challenged, I pointed him to the automated university phonebook, trying hard not to hang up. Ron persisted. He said he had heard about a class project I had done and that I had been selected for a very competitive internship at IBM. It took me a few minutes to grasp that he was not pulling a fast one on me and accept his offer before he changed his mind. I spent many months in Austin working at IBM before coming back for my second semester at Madison.

Before the second semester ended, I was pretty miserable as a teaching assistant, a job I had to take because no other research lab would accept me for a paid position. With two classes to teach, lectures to attend and research on top of that, I found myself suddenly disliking my circumstances. I did not mind the hours; what I did not understand was the unfairness in pay and access to paid opportunities for research. There were times when I locked myself inside the women's restroom, crying. I found myself growing rapidly discontented with the people I encountered. I couldn't understand why I felt that way. I was, after all, among my heroes in academia. Heroes who had written papers I had read, on research, on life; who maintained that passion and hard work outweighed bookish wisdom. In their rhetoric, they applauded the rebels, those who looked past regurgitating facts on exam sheets, those that pursued the ends of a problem. I had embraced that attitude as an undergraduate and then during my master's. I was finally at their doorstep, but my heart was not happy. Getting into research groups suddenly seemed almost impossible. Professors were less concerned with my track record and more concerned with shepherding the team-players. I told myself I could be a team-player. I took to working on one or two problems that were interesting to me, without pay.

While in Raleigh, I had Ann to laugh with at our bald lecturers' most famous antic: talking to our chest instead of making eye-contact. Here I had no one to talk to. Aurora was in Nijmegen on a short trip. We exchanged emails regularly, including some late-night haiku contests – she would send me a haiku and I had to respond within the hour. All my time seemed to be spent staring at a computer monitor. For many days I did not open my mouth at Madison, but I often reminded myself, 'I need to be a team-player. I am one of the guys, I will get there.'

A positive outcome of this unhappiness was that I threw myself headfirst into physical activity. This included swimming, cycling, running, walking, or cooking and then washing dishes. I rode my bike all over town, very often through the arboretum and out to a network of quieter roads behind it. In Madison, riding a bike was a political badge of sorts. Meanwhile, my buddy Eddie from Purdue, who had been a part of the ROTC (a reserve corps of student officers in the US Marines) to pay college tuition, had gone off to war. None of us understood what for, except that there was oil involved. It felt liberating to ride a bike rather than a car as a personal rebellion against the use of oil. I was completely frustrated with the way things were going with my research, the news with Eddie, and a seeming lack of direction in my life. I was also running more than ever before. I remember running for many hours one day, completely lost in my own world. When I showed up at home, my mother, who was visiting, was taken aback. Not only had I been out running for several hours, I was covered with dried-up salt, from all the sweat. My mother noticed that something was amiss. I had been in Madison for almost a year and a half. I had stopped calling my family. Before she left to return to Bangalore, I had confessed to her that I had borrowed money to pay the previous month's rent, as my salary had not been enough to cover it, after I'd bought my bike. As most Indian parents might, she told me she would take care of it, but I refused. For once, she did not insist. She could see that it was important for me to find my own truths.

After the second year, I moved in with Alicia, who held one of the two coveted fellowships in the computer sciences department. She was bright, funny in an understated way, loved books, played an instrument, and was instrumental in resurrecting my Scrabble addiction even though I often ended up losing 4-2 to her at speed Scrabble. Neither of us got along with the rest of the crowd in computer science and engineering. Believing that we had miraculously found each other, when in reality it was inevitable given the few women in the PhD programme, we hung out together at home, drank a lot of tea, and helped each other sort out any problems in our assignments or research. I was not happy being by myself and having a roommate really helped me tide over those difficult days. Soon after moving in with Alicia, I would make a lot more friends because I was suddenly more confident in seeking them out. I met a lot of people who loved swimming, cycling and running and made an effort to join them on group workouts, many of which started before 5.30 a.m. I also started dating a runner, who was working towards a PhD in liberal arts. I could not keep up with him on our runs but being with him brought me joy. He was the version of myself I wished I could be. He was studying food banks and urban poverty. I found his meticulous approach to research as endearing as his desire to spend time with me, doing the most mundane things. Shopping for groceries, strolling hand-in-hand in the evenings or running. He was a breath of fresh air compared to the engineers I was surrounded by, all very sure of themselves and talking a mile a minute.

I continued working at the same research lab in the computer science department for almost a year. They regularly hired PhD students from engineering, where I was enrolled, but there seemed no hope that I would be taken up as a full-time research assistant. One day, after teaching all my classes and feeling thoroughly miserable because I couldn't muster up the energy to start my research work, I found my mind wandering. I wondered if there were other women who had gone through similar turmoil in the past. With that thought in mind, I looked up the statistics for the women who had graduated from the computer science department over the past decade and found that it was less than

7 per cent of the entire graduating set! When I approached the dean with this data, just to put things in perspective and convince him that I deserved a chance at a paid research assistantship, he smelled a lawsuit and refused to talk to me any further. I tried to reason with him that in case a PhD was not possible, I should at least be allowed to leave with a master's degree in computer science because I was two classes away from completing the coursework that rendered me eligible for it. Both of us knew that the degree would be of no use to me since I already had a master's from North Carolina. I just wanted to mark my time in Madison with a meaningful bookend. But he refused. I was confused. This guy was Indian, he had gone to one of the IITs in India, and he was a legend. He belonged to a group of professors I idolized, but what he did next brought all that crashing down. After our conversation ended, he walked out and into the elevator, but when I walked in after him, he turned around and walked out again because he didn't want to ride down with me. I burst out laughing at how stupid I had been, reading what people wrote and believing they actually lived what they preached.

My discontentment had made me realize that I probably wanted to quit my PhD, but I did not want to admit it to myself. My alternative to graduate school, which I was not convinced about, was to run a business. I had worked on a small idea for a product, once I graduated from Purdue. Being in an academic space where delusions ran high, I always thought I had more time and energy than I actually did. The truth is that I faced more failure than success in the first three years. I was always too busy to build the product I had in mind and I had no resources to speak of. In the light of my new situation, with a PhD seeming well out of reach, I decided to head to San Diego to scope out a trade conference and see what the potential for a small consulting business would be.

San Diego was magic. Encouraged by my boyfriend, I raced a local half-marathon the weekend before the trade show, at Carlsbad. The night before, I shared a meal with a couple of runners, called Paul and Roger, who updated me on their own revolution against the establishment by not cutting their hair to the 2.5 inches that was needed for the basketball team, stripping to their jockstraps and shoes thereof, and quitting in a stand against 'the man'. There were a few Volkswagons and road trips thrown in as well. Thirty years had passed since they were freshmen, but we struck up a great conversation. As I ran the crowded race with 7,000 people, in what resembled a washing machine without the water, I saw some signs that said Jesus would save my soul. I turned to a fellow runner and said, 'Geez, I am going to be late for church.' He didn't get it, of course. At mile 10, I had to take off my singlet and race number as the pin I had used to fasten the number had snapped and was cutting through my skin. I wondered whether running in Bangalore in only a sports bra and shorts would be blasphemous. I was trying to catch mile 11, knowing that miles 12 and 13 would reel me in. Two hours and nine minutes later, the finish line was a blur, but I was pleased.

My quest on that trip to the West Coast was learning how to say *Amor Vincit Omnia* (Love Conquers All), because it felt like my life had no love left in it. My love for the keyboard was an occupational hazard but my love for love was a mental problem I didn't seem to be able to get rid of. All my pursuits were underlined by love, a fierce love for solving problems, for understanding concepts, for working hard on assignments, completing a hard run, swim or bike ride. Love was the beginning and the end for me. Madison was testing my resilience in a bad way – I felt crippled and my voice felt muffled, almost weak.

My first day at the trade show started on a high note. One that seemed to say, 'Don't give up on mankind yet, Anu, there is hope.' This set off a series of smiling-to-myself episodes, or as my buddy Aurora once put it, a deer-in-headlights sort of look, as I took on the 3,000-odd attendees at the human zoo of this conference. I knew I stood out in the crowd because of my saree. I felt relaxed for the first time in a long time. I ran into a Canadian called Pierre and struck up a conversation about Canada and the business and his two kids. I had always been madly in love with Canadians because free healthcare loomed on the horizon and hippydom seemed to be genetically inherited. There were several parties with endless networking. The news was very good overall for the trade in general and for my company in particular.

On the final night, I set out looking for Pierre, to bid adieu to him and his partner. And tell them that though their cars did not start in the Ottawa winter, they were inspiring in their verbose love for someplace called home – what did that mean, exactly?

The question on everyone's mind that night was either 'Where is the Wonderbread factory?' which was the location at which the last supper was being hosted, or 'Are you going to the Wonderbread factory?' A huge set of baseball fans had just checked out of Petco Park and were also making their way in that general direction. One more round in the human zoo saw me bid farewell to all my newfound friends, after which I hopped into a cab for the short ride back to my hotel. The cab driver answered, 'No automatic!' to the question 'Where are you from?', making me giggle like a three-year-old. I had an overwhelming feeling that I was about to lose something. The warm summer night, the uphill turns to Ash Avenue and the murky dark sky seemed to conspire together to make my lasting friendships in Madison impossible. The cabbie, in the meantime, kept sighing and placing his chin on his free hand every stoplight we hit. Was he secretly the Marvin from the *Hitchhikers Guide*? Who knew? I couldn't sleep that night and went on a long stroll through the Gaslamp Quarter. I realized that I loved San Diego because to me, in one word, it was *frumpy.*

I walked until midnight, alone with my thoughts. My life was in a rut and while I was doing my best, the lifestyle was wearing me out. I realized that I missed my folks terribly. They formed a big part of the way in which I saw the world and its coasts. Once I got back to my room, I wrote to one of my best friends in Madison, Dan, at 3 a.m. and told him that I expected a twenty-page essay on the funniest incident he remembered from high school that involved a woman with red hair, a poodle that was in love with his shoe laces, and a guitar case. Suddenly, I felt I was getting closer to an answer. Here is what he wrote:

Ahhh, yes. The girl with the red hair, I remember her like it was yesterday. I remember how she used to walk past me in the halls of that dungeon of so-called higher education as though I didn't exist; all the while the scent of 'Eternity' that she adorned on her sweet milky skin (which usually reminded me of cat litter) made my adolescent soul scream for this charade to end.

I knew that she longed for me the same way I for her. She would strut past me in the hallway, me in my Levi 501 button-fly blues, Chuck Taylor canvas high tops (red and slightly pointing inward) and a t-shirt which advertised a product known as 'SEX WAX' and her in the ever-so-revealing white button-up oxford, bottom ends tied up so as to reveal her beautiful belly button (I never remembered what else she was wearing). I knew that she could see me, I knew that she could feel the same heat that was generated by me strumming my 'six string' as she strutted past me, on her way to the 'girls room' to check her lip gloss. Her name was 'Cherry'.

I knew she would be mine; I knew my gentle notes were slowly sinking into her inner depths; convincing her that she eventually wouldn't be able to hold out; that one day she would break, throw me against a locker in the gymnasium locker room, and kiss me ever so passionately until neither one of us could breathe. That day was coming soon.

I just had to get past the dog. You see, every time I approached her house (which incidentally was right across the street from school) I was attacked by the 'poodle'. This crazy little dog with little white 'puffs' at the bottom of his legs, end of his tail, and a big one atop his head, was sent by the elderly lady next door to attack me every time I approached Cherry's house. Or that was my theory.

You see, I was convinced that the old lady thought that I was perhaps carrying some sort of bomb in my guitar case; or perhaps a 'weapon of mass destruction'. She would glare at me while I passed by her yard, meanwhile hanging her large, wet knickers on the line to dry, disdain in her eyes. She had it in for me and I had to find a plan – a plan to get around her and her silly little cream puff of a dog.

(This is where, sadly, I run out of time to finish writing, what I think, is a beautifully composed story so far, so I need to end it fast.)

Funny how things work out … in the end, I realize that this girl was a little out of my league. That is to say that, she was one of those 'Molly Ringwald' types that expects you to pay for everything, go to medical school, buy her Gucci luggage and spa retreats in the Mediterranean; all the while sipping Piña Coladas while you're giving some guy you don't even know a prostate exam and dreaming of the egg salad sandwich you're going to be eating at lunch. No thanks.

However, I did come out on top with the dog. I finally realized that the dog was actually after my shoelaces. Two years prior, when my Himalayan cat Muffy passed away in a freak accident involving a mouse trap and a camera (long story), my Mother wanted so badly to 'take away my pain' (yeah, right … pain), that she had some shoelaces custom made for me with hemp and … well … Muffy's fur. Sick, huh. But, had I not worn them, I would have let on the fact that I really wasn't that upset about the dumb cat and maybe wouldn't have gotten the new computer which I also received for my 'pain and suffering'. Like taking candy from a baby.

Anyway, so the next time this dog 'attacks' me, the old hag isn't around. Right before 'Randy' reaches me, I pull open my empty guitar case, he jumps at me; hits the inside of the case, I close the case and I'm outta there.

Three years and a few hundred Scooby Snacks later, my man 'Randy' has taken 'Best in Show' four times and barks at old ladies who pass my house. As for Cherry, well, she's married to a guy who unclogs toilets for a living and has three kids all living in their beautiful trailer in Stoughton, WI. Randy is retired and we are living in the Mediterranean on the $750,000 he's won in prize money. Isn't life sweet?

After coming back to Madison, one evening, lost in thought about what I should do, I heard my roommate walking in the door. She looked a bit dazed, I thought she was just tired. She plopped down on the couch and said, 'Weird thing is, today, I could not understand a word in my research group's presentation. I did not agree with a single inference the guy was making but I didn't have the heart to say anything.' We spoke at length about how several of our classmates seemed to nod their heads or agree with the popular theories. Later in my life, I would figure out that corridors of influence are populated by like-minded individuals, all brainwashed by the same academic systems and ideologies. If you don't agree with the crowd, you are unlikely to have a rosy path ahead of you. A few months later, both my roommate and I quit our PhDs. She took a job in New York and I decided to return home to Bangalore. If I didn't develop a spine at the age of twenty-three, I never would.

BACK TO THE FUTURE

Brown Girl in the Ring

'Cause I'm all alone
There's no one here beside me
My problems have all gone
There's no one to deride me!
But ya gotta have friends...
—Donkey, *Shrek*

I am often asked how I trained for my first Ironman. At the outset, I must clarify that an active childhood, hours of cycling in college, and a healthy dose of emotional support from my parents were foundational to my success. When I started to train for an Ironman in earnest, I was enamoured by the difficulty of the race. The thought of training in my own backyard had all the makings of a huge adventure. That seemingly impossible goal, which over time becomes the air you breathe, which drives you forward, gives your imagination wings – that became my lifeline. There was no fame or fortune associated with it. It was simply about doing what I loved and doing it well. I have never defined my place in life by competing with anyone or anything, and my goals did not include actively redefining any cultural stereotypes. Sport simply gave me the perfect outlet to focus my energy and allowed me to cultivate an understanding of where I lived. I was able to rediscover my neighbourhood, understand which roads led where and what was really happening outside our doors, by engaging in a different way. Without realizing it, I also obtained an education second to none, by doing something on my own terms.

In early 2006, I went on a short visit to New Zealand, where I had been invited by a new client who was setting up a business in India. Booking tickets to Christchurch had been more challenging than I thought – I was wrought with anxiety because I was not sure I wanted to leave home for long stretches again. The three people I loved were in Bangalore, I didn't need much more to make me happy. Finally, Father helped me decide to make the journey. Since I couldn't afford a fancy hotel, I opted to stay in a lodge with affordable weekly rates. I had made my enquiries and the location seemed ideally close to all the places I needed to get to.

New Zealand was ahead of India by eight hours, so most of the meetings with my client were set up in the afternoons, when he could also talk to the rest of my team in Bangalore.

On the second day of my stay, I encountered a coach who mistook me for one of his group of athletes; it turned out they were all staying at the same lodge. He caught me lying down, eating outdated soda crackers I had bought for a dollar on sale, with Vegemite, a Kiwi specialty, and reading *A Confederacy of Dunces*. The next thing I knew, I was being snapped at: 'You did not come here to read books, you came here to get fit. Put that down and go for a run!' If he had not been as good-looking as he was, I might have given it back to him. Instead, I decided not to correct his impression and went on a run. I had nothing to do till 4 p.m. New Zealand time, anyway.

I would later find out that the coach came from a very humble background and overcame all sorts of adversity to pursue his true passion, sport. The group of athletes were training for Ironman New Zealand. Axel Anders, Birger Andersson, Carl Dagmar and Dag Decanter were from Norway and there were two Americans – Kristy Lachlan, a triathlete, and a runner who insisted we only address him by his initials, 'CBD'. Then there were Brianna Adamson and David Cameron from England, and me, the lone Indian. It was a mismatched potpourri in every way. Axel was super-loud, constantly comparing Ironman to giving birth, and was hung up on American culture via repeat viewings of *Seinfeld*. Kristy was angry about something, but our common love for the movie *Napolean Dynamite* meant we hit it off very soon. She was dating Carl, who kept quizzing me about *Indian Idol*. Dag had tagged along with Axel and was the only person I could keep up with.

I briefly fashioned myself as the coach's latest protégé – a few weeks couldn't kill me, I thought, and sportingly tagged along on many training sessions with the other athletes. From them I learned about the various corporations and federations that ran the sport. In those remarkable weeks, I also pulled up my socks and signed up for a half Ironman in Auckland, finishing in 8 hours and 45 minutes and having a near-death experience because I was so friggin' exhausted. Right before I left New Zealand, I also ran my first marathon, at Motatapu, in five-and-a-half hours. The off-road marathon that started at a sheep station at Glendhu Bay, in Wanaka, included some serious climbing, almost 600 metres, before descending into Arrowtown. It was a point-to-point race and that made sense to me. I predicted that I would probably finish my first Ironman in right around the cut-off time of seventeen hours. But after the marathon, which was a doozy, I was unable to do my laundry for several days. My multi-cultural roommates, as helpful as ever, took charge and I could only hope that all the giggling in the laundry room had nothing to do with my trendy twosome of oversized cotton underwear and EOR pyjamas, both of which I had bought on sale in Madison. We believed in dressing comfortably back then.

On the flight home, I had a daydream about my brief time in New Zealand. I dreamt that after several years of excessive exercise and a steady diet of spinach and apples and more spinach, I managed to get really fast on the bike. I also had thin thighs.

Back in present time, I wrote down my favourite one-liners from the trip.

Axel: 'Anu, if you swim any slower, you'll sink.'

Birger: 'These are biking bibs for f*@!'s sake', in response to my calling his biking shorts 'weird' for having suspenders.

Brianna: 'What is wrong with today', in response to my statement about working hard 'next week'.

Kristy: 'Anu, you cannot ride Zippy in your Ironman, it is not a road bike and there IS a difference!'

David: '...'

Carl: 'I like shorts with pink baby elephants.'

CBD: '... right.'

Dag: '... yjhust take it easa' – which, in English, was 'just take it easy'.

The coach's side-kick: 'I have a member of the MTV generation right here.'

After what seemed like months of training in Bangalore, a few weeks before my planned Ironman race in Canada, in August 2006, I took the cheapest flight from Bangalore to Montreal. I planned on training in Ottawa for a few weeks, get myself a decent bike, and see what I could do in an Ironman. I had about US$2,000 in my pocket, having wiped out the rest of my earnings.

Once in Canada, in August 2006, I procured a new pink Trek bike, which was on sale, and promptly named her Mrs Martinez. The purchase depleted my cash reserve by $700 and left me with $1,300 for the next four weeks. I moved into a house that cost $500 a month, with a roommate. I was a little disturbed on the third day when, after realizing that I was a triathlete training for her first Ironman, my roommate put up a newspaper clip about a cyclist who was run over on the roads nearby. I ignored this, but she seemed determined to rain on my party, even complaining about my getting the floor in the shower cubicle wet. I said timidly, 'But that part of the house is bound to accumulate latent moisture and I cannot avoid it.' She backed off temporarily but after a week, we had another brilliant conversation that sealed my fate.

Roommate: 'So, like I was saying, you are training for a triathlon. I have so many other things to do. I have seen swimmers, Olympic athletes, professional athletes. All can still balance life and sport ... but you came from India to Canada for a sport? Who does that?'

Me: 'I'm sorry, did you say you have lived with swimmers who went up to the Olympics?'

Roommate: 'No, I have not lived with them. My master's coach almost made it to the Olympics.'

Me: 'You swim with a master's team? When?'

Roommate: 'Well, the whole week before the sprint race I did with my sister, I swam master's, with an Olympic coach.'

I tried to be compassionate and understand her world-view on all the ways in which I had let the universe down, but I had to train. Although I was living in a great neighbourhood with manicured lawns and losing almost a month's rent was hard, I decided to move out. As my dear mom would have said, my mind was more important than money, any day of the week.

I moved into a cheap hostel that cost $17 a night, where I had to share a room with five other people. We slept on bunk beds and shared a common kitchen where all groceries were kept, labelled and jealously guarded. My roommates were intriguing characters. One was a long-haired man from the Dakotas who claimed to be a pagan witch; another was a leather-loving tattooed woman who was a bounty hunter by day and a writer by night. Then there was a runaway from Iowa who worked at a local restaurant chain, Hardees, and wore thick glasses; a muscular bouncer at a downtown bar; and a college dropout funded by his mother, in search of the next great artistic debut. This colourful company made me want to stay outside the hostel for as long as I could. Not that I didn't want to get to know my hostel-mates better, but I had several questions about my own identity swimming in my head, so I thought it best to enjoy the solitude, traffic-free, while I could.

My routine in Ottawa consisted of a long swim in the mornings, several hours of riding at Gatineau Park, a meagre lunch, a nap in the park, and a run in the evenings. I explored the surrounding areas of French Canada on my bike. It was nearing fall and the trees were on fire. Maple trees and cedars were aplenty, as were birds, and I once spotted a beaver. On my many all-day outings, I would chat with the trees. Sometimes, they laughed at my outfit, and other times at my crazy cycling stunts. Mostly, they kept me in my place and whispered to me about perseverance. At one such important tree-person summit, while I was harbouring several doubts about what I was doing in Ottawa, I asked the trees silently, 'I am in Canada to race a triathlon. Isn't this too far to come for a hobby? Is this a hobby? Don't you think it's way out there?' The trees replied, also silently, *Well, we are in the Outouais region ... yes, it is way Outouais there.* And saying so, they seemed to snicker amongst themselves. The breeze that emanated was a small relief, given that it was a four-hour-ride day. I said, 'Very funny! I am asking a serious question.' The reply came right back: *Well, you are getting a serious answer. What is wrong with living an inspired life? Would you rather get married?* I said, 'Hell no!' To calm me down, they said, *Hey, do you know who visits Gatineau Park ever so often?* I said, 'No.' They said, *The common loon ... so you are in good company.* They seemed to snicker again and, slightly miffed but laughing aloud, I rode out, done and happy for the day.

I had set myself a budget for food. I would eat a breakfast of oatmeal or bread at the hostel, splurge on lunch at a Subway, and eat Ramen for dinner. As someone put it, the goal was to maximize intake of the most calories, per cent spent on food. Potatoes, as it turned out, were the cheapest source of nutrition. There were fries for a dollar or slightly more, Pringles chips that came with enough salt to revive any loss of electrolytes and then, of course, there were the famous servings of mashed potatoes with every sit-down meal I treated myself to. I thought of my parents often on the longer days. They may not have lived in hostels or counted calories, but they faced very real challenges. Once I was done training at the end of the day, I would go to the public library in Ottawa to answer work emails with any remaining brain cells I had that were still functioning.

My longest ride until I reached Canada had been a 180-km ride, to Mysore and beyond. I outdid myself by doing a longer ride to Kingston, a neighbouring town. I set off with a map (we did not have Google Maps back then), directions from the local bike shop and a fully charged phone. I was on the TransCanada trail, which was made of several smaller community trails, connected to provide a recreational path. My goal was to simulate race conditions and ride through without too many stops. I had to learn to eat and drink on my bike. I had to keep my wits about me because unlike an actual race-course, there was traffic in some sections.

I have had many epiphanies in my life, but a string of them hit me in quick succession on that ride. My peers were chasing different milestones. Most were married. They had started families. They had career goals and they worked 'real jobs', as they liked to remind me. Most of my relatives, my brother included, thought my business was a hobby. I had the tough task of breaking out of my parents' shell, which I had never intended to inhabit in the first place. Like every other girl in India, I have a coterie of overly smart aunts and uncles with an opinion on everything: I was too old for marriage, too young to try to build a company, too thin with all the running I was doing, too fat when I was a child, too fast when moving all over the United States and quitting my PhD unlike 'a good Iyer girl', and too slow to learn the fine art of making choice Indian desserts to attract 'a good Iyer boy' who would save me from myself. My parents did not speak of it to me, but my relatives put intense pressure on them to find me a man so I could 'settle down'. What are Indian women anyway? Sediment? Settling is so boring.

My own milestones involved looking at the number 200 on my bike computer, after having ridden that many kilometres. I asked myself if this was a worthy goal. The granular chutzpah that accompanied me most times was replaced by a lesson in pain and patience on that ride to Kingston. No matter how good you look, you still have to work very hard to become good at anything. I remember telling someone I met that I would be very sad if I did not meet my athletic goals before I died. But it would make me sadder to not be independent. Being an independent woman let me earn money on my own terms, to feed my somewhat instinctive addiction to wanderlust.

The green fields resembled endless rows of emeralds. Mrs Martinez and I had nothing to prove to anybody. We were two lone rangers on the road. Anyone who wanted to join us was welcome on the ride, just as anyone who found us silly was welcome to leave. One of the songs Janis Joplin sang, '*Me and Bobby McGee*', is about her travels, her love for music, and her love for a boy called Bobby McGee, who slips away. I thought, in the case of Mrs Martinez and me, we had slipped away from our men because the road seemed too tantalizing to not explore. Not the other way around.

At the end of the ride, I found myself in front of a library on a college campus in Kingston, Ontario. All I knew was that the rooms were cheap, breakfast was free, and it was right next to the lake that I was hoping to swim in before riding back on Sunday. I have always loved libraries – they are the epicentre of all things idealistic and impossible in this world, encouraging free speech, true love and equality. Libraries loved me back with the order, silence and solitude they brought to my life. Have you ever been in a library right at opening time? No one is in yet, and the heady scent of books overwhelms your senses. Quiet corners turn with words from musty books playing hopscotch as you try to decide which book to borrow. The librarian looks at you through her glasses and smiles with that familiar, benevolent 'you again' look.

Standing outside that library in Kingston brought back memories from Purdue – all those hours at the Siegesmund Engineering Library, solving equations on neat sheets of paper. Spending stolen moments at the Humanities Library, just looking at great works of literature, knowing there was no time to read them all. Hiding out at the Math Library when I did not want people to find me. In Madison, spending countless hours at the twenty-four-hour College Library close to Lake Mendota, the Law School Library in Bascom Hall and the Memorial Library on State Street. These spaces had been sacred to me, in my time as a student. I realized I harboured no resentment over the way things had turned out at graduate school, because I was smiling, looking at that big library before me.

The turnstile leading into the library appeared symbolic to me. It seemed to be the gateway to a continuum between the didactic and the dynamic. As opposed to the comforting act of reading a book, solving a problem or writing a report, which came more naturally to me, standing outside the library I felt as if I were in a new world, one that came with hours and hours of physical toil. Maybe my bike seat was the perfect Parthenon for slightly sweaty, alternative forms of prayer. I had ridden a long way the day before, from Ottawa to Kingston. Temperatures had ranged between 21 and 29 degrees Celsius for the most part. My brown skin was burnt to a shade I had never seen before. The prize was fresh air, sunshine and solitude. I spent that night out in town, with a margarita that was way too sweet and in the company of strangers. I had come to love my adventure, not to mention the whole new experience of feeling my ribs. From being a chubby nerd who couldn't fathom cliquish jocks, I had become someone who thought, why walk to the library when you can run?

Triskaidekaphobia

Ayi jagadamba madamba kadamba vanapriya vaasini haasarate
Shikhari shiromani tunga Himaalaya shringa nijaalaya
madhyagate

‖ 3.1: Salutations to the Mother of the Universe, Who is My
Own Mother,
Who Likes to Live in the Forest of Kadamba Trees and Delight
in Laughter and Mirth,
3.2: Whose Abode is in the Middle of the Crest-Jewel of Peaks
of the Lofty Himalayas ‖

—Durga Stotram, Devi Mahtmyam

My first Ironman was pretty special and unforgettable for several reasons, one of them being the many fashion faux pas I executed to the T with regard to nutrition and clothing. On race day, I woke up at 3 a.m. and scrambled to get some breakfast. The night before the race, I had taken a luxurious detour from my hostel saga in Ottawa and decided to stay in a private room. As the prehistoric microwave in the common kitchen cooked my cereal, grunting with the effort, I poured myself a cup of coffee and went over a mental checklist. I panicked briefly when I realized that I couldn't remember if it was a teaspoon or tablespoon of salt that I needed to add to my drinking water. So I made two bottles, one with a teaspoon and the other with a tablespoon – which was bigger than a soup spoon but, oh well, I didn't go to finishing school. At 4 a.m., I got into a phone booth and dialled home. My mother sang out 'Best of luck! Best of luck! Best of luck!' and my father said 'Best of luck!' after which he had to add two more when my mother and I gasped in horror and chided him. We believe in the holy grail of the triumvirate, my mother and I. Things-in-threes make sense to us. She happens to be an intellectual property lawyer and in Indian courts, the judges say 'Order! Order! Order!', or so Bollywood would have us believe. I am a triathlete. We have to swim, bike and run, because one sport is simply not good enough.

At 4.30 a.m., I took a cab to the start line. The cabbie was very annoyed that my bike-grease was messing up his car seat. I was yelled at in Arabic about my bike, or my perfume, or both. I really could not tell.

The cabbie's anger flummoxed me, but it was too early in the day to yell back. In my hurry to leave, I forgot my bottles in the cab. When I got to the race site, it was pitch black. The darkness did not intimidate me anymore; I was used to it from training in Bangalore, week after week. It was a good thing that I couldn't see much, because I had no clue that I was vastly under-dressed. I had put on my short flannel pyjamas and a nice bike jersey to hold all my nutrition for the ride. I had resisted the temptation to buy *proper* race gear because I just did not see how I could wear spandex to work, and anyway, finances were tight. I put on my second-hand wetsuit, begged a volunteer to find me two bottles of electrolyte, and got into the water for a quick warm-up. It was time for the swim to start and I was excited and ready to have a great race.

I thought of my training misadventures in Bangalore as I warmed up in the water. The swim coach, the friendly neighbourhood relay-dogs, the toilets, my mother and our girly secrets, my father and his never-say-die attitude, my brother, my clueless friends. All of them were part of the journey that had brought me to the start line. There had been plenty of strife just getting through the day-to-day training. But I took it as a bonus: maybe friction was the only way to start a fire. I hugged myself and a few others, furiously tried to channel my inner nimble-footed-sitar-player-self, said a silent prayer along the lines of 'Cheers, all of you who said I couldn't. Amma, Appa, you are my blue sky. This one's for you.' And off we went.

The water was calm that morning. Dawn was barely breaking when we warmed up, but once the swim was underway, I could see the line of buoys clearly. I started strong, for I had been able to swim with greater consistency at Ottawa's public pools. By the turnaround, I realized that I had been swimming much faster than I had expected to. I paid the price as I got a little tired towards the end of the swim and could no longer see the buoys. Exiting the water in 1 hour and 20 minutes, way quicker than I had imagined, I had to fight to get my wetsuit off. I didn't know the tricks of transition then, and I still don't. After what seemed like ten minutes, I got on my bike, feeling psyched. The bike course had many, many loops of the same loop. I was eating as well as I could, drinking water and moving my pedals to the best of my abilities.

I termed this portion of the race the *Barbiturate Breakeven*, because it involved 180 km of riding and I had to stay awake. It gave me plenty of time to think, and somewhere along the way I realized I had become a new fan of the English letter 'b'. It was the beginning of a number of cool words. Baker, Bowden and Brianna, three legendary triathlete women. Bangalore, the love of my life. Blonde, which I momentarily wished I were then, for Birger, the uber-biker, who no doubt preferred blondes. Balanced, although I never figured out what that meant. Bombastic. And most importantly, buxom. My receding chest, owing to hours and hours of exercise, had been a matter of great concern to me. As long as I was in engineering school, that was the only thing that had got me noticed.

Riding along, I felt like a denizen in a land where the streets had no names. You know that feeling when you are riding home and your worst nightmare about someone swapping all the street signs comes true? Well, as far as naming streets goes, Indians have way more than a dozen languages to choose from. If I thought 'merica offered too many choices and roads to run on, I had even more waiting for me back home. I was free to pursue what I pleased, with self-respect and independence. I felt elated by that thought.

The bike ride took almost seven hours. I was a little bored by the time I got off my bike and happy to put on my running shoes. This was a small race in Canada and did not come with the silly rules that some other races impose on their overpaying participants, so we were allowed to use Walkmans. My companion was a CD player that I had packed into my transition bag. Since it was a four-loop run, I picked it up along with my blue running pouch, stocked with extra batteries, just in case. This time, my trusty blue pouch had Mars bars instead of toffees. After running the first 10 km, I decided I would get some Coke to drink at the next aid station. Much to my dismay, the volunteers refused to hand me a bottle. I thought I had run past them too fast and should have slowed down. I kept running, hoping for better luck at the next aid station. But the pattern continued at four more rest stops, until I had run almost half the marathon. That's when a light-bulb came on in my head. Attired in my flannel pants, two layers of Salvation Army sweaters to keep from freezing on the run, my blue waist-pouch and antiquated CD player, I must have looked like a jogger in the park. I had to stop at the following aid station and lift up all my layers of clothing to show them the race number pinned to my jersey, to convince them to part with the precious black sugar water. I was annoyed that I had to stop but I was dying at this point, so I had no choice. I ran the marathon in 4 hours and 23 minutes flat, ending my first Ironman with a huge smile.

I didn't hang around after the race because I had no family there. I didn't know anyone, except the volunteer community and the locals who had come to cheer, and they didn't know me, so the ending was anticlimactic. It was lonely, to be precise. I walked back to the swim start and took a dip in the lake. I wanted to cool off and give my muscles a break. The race had started and ended for me within thirteen hours: 12 hours and 42 minutes of racing and eighteen minutes of transitioning. The number thirteen seemed serendipitous. Mangalam-paati and my mom were big fans of the Devi Mahatmyam, which tells the story of our sacred feminine goddesses. That had thirteen chapters too, if I recalled correctly, and they took you through the process of awakening, conquering demons and obliterating doubt. I concluded that Goddess Durga was one hell of a woman, and I was fortunate to have centuries of tradition behind me – to be inspired by and contest. I thanked the water, the wind and the roads, packed up my things and called for a taxi to take me back to the hostel.

That night, I walked back to the same phone booth and called my mother to tell her I had finished. She let out a loud, excited whoop. The same kind of whoop she lets out when she spies a lizard in the living room, or a cockroach, or both. It was LOUD. My father said, 'Kanna, I was thinking of you all day.' I said, 'I was thinking of you all day too.' My brother added his congratulations. Before he could say anything more, my mother grabbed the phone and said, '*Saaptiya di?*' (Did you eat?) Luckily for me, it was late on a Saturday night, and except for a few drunken revellers, there was no one around to be startled by the sight of an Indian woman simultaneously bawling and laughing hysterically inside a plastic box.

The morning after the Ironman began with a laconic and lasting laziness, the kind of day that wakes you with a feeling of gentle heat on the back of your neck. Then it begins to burn, but you're feeling so deliciously lazy that you don't care to do anything about it. I was mostly just numb and pondering my next steps. What I had accomplished was empowering. Enigmatic. You name it, and the adjective probably held true. The fact that the world was not represented in the World Championships was not going to change soon, I reasoned. This sport, not unlike baseball, primarily defined the world as North America. I felt a bit like a bazooka, a shoulder missile – I was literally uplifted on the shoulders of my strong family, the wonderful women that surrounded me – my mother's sisters, my best friends, my mother herself, and memories of my grandmothers. Not once in my long trials on race-day had I thought of my professors or the need for compliance that so greatly bothered me in the halls of academia. 'Bullshit,' I thought to myself. The Goo Goo Dolls wrote, 'And everything you're chasing, it seems to leave you empty.' I had felt like that when I left Madison. But since my failures at graduate school, I had started to want a little less emotion and a little more action. I was living life on the offensive, rather than the defensive. It had been tough to set the Ironman as a goal. I had not talked about it, even to my parents. I knew my friends in Bangalore would never understand, and I lived in constant fear of rebuke. I was no revolutionary, I loved to belong. I just didn't know where I belonged. For the time being, I decided to enjoy my very private victory in finishing a difficult race.

Sitting in a dorm the following Friday, in Montreal, my flight out being on Sunday evening, I was hit by sudden anxiety. I was not sure when I would be able to return to Canada. This trip had set me back financially. I had a grand total of $100 in my purse, and I intended to use half of that for a luxury taxi that could house both me and my bike.

I panicked, too, because leaving Canada would mean no more racing. In India, a marathon can vary from 4 km to 10 km to 21.1 km to 42.2 km. As I sat there thinking, the 'buy one, get one free' mentality took over – I suppose I am more Indian than I care to admit – and I registered for the Montreal Marathon that weekend. It was best to train as much as I could, whenever I could. I was staying in yet another hostel, where I had the top bunk-bed. I felt so claustrophobic that I woke up at 3 a.m. I ran down to the start line at about 7 a.m., admiring the pre-race stretching routines of various people. I noticed a few people dressed in Energizer Bunny outfits, carrying flags with numbers on them: 4.30, 3.30, 3.00. I wondered what they meant. I assumed it had something to do with bib numbers, but I couldn't have cared less. My flight to Bangalore would leave within ten hours of the start of the marathon and I had to hurry. I finished the race in 4 hours and 20 minutes. I had started out next to the group whose flag read '3.20', without realizing that the big, annoying, furry bunny with an energizer drum was a pace bunny. In trying to get away from it, I ran out too hard. I paid the price for it by having to request a wheelchair to get my rear end on the plane back to Bangalore, after travelling to the airport by bus. In retrospect, running a marathon the weekend following my Ironman debut was probably not the smartest thing to do. But on that entire flight back from Montreal to Bangalore, my smile was bigger than the Cheshire cat's could have ever been.

An Inheritance O'Floss

...love must surely reside in the gap between desire and fulfillment, in the lack, not the contentment.
— *The Inheritance of Loss*, Kiran Desai

Returning to Bangalore from Ottawa after my first Ironman, I told a couple of my friends what I had done. They were very proud of my achievement. I felt good, wrote about it in my journal and moved on. My mother was secretly glad when my tan vanished, but she embraced my new path with as much enthusiasm as she had any other. She helped me find new and healthier recipes that suited my dietary requirements. I had sworn my family to secrecy from extended family and neighbours. In doing so, I excluded even the relatives I loved. I was dying to show off to my favourite maternal uncle, Chidambaram, and two of my maternal aunts, Sacchu and Sambu, but I resisted. I knew that it was not respectful to keep secrets in the extended family, but I really did not want to invite opinions from my aunts and uncles, who did not approve of my choices.

I made friends with the early hours of the morning: 5.30 a.m. in Bangalore was definitely a time high on delusions, straight out of a Bond movie, with fast cars zipping along the major roads. Headlights, dust and grime were present in equal measure to confuse the senses. I dressed very conservatively when I trained outdoors in Bangalore. In fact, on my runs, I often felt like a Kathakali dancer in full costume. One unfortunate morning, a costume malfunction rendered me flat on my face, some two hours into training. This was one of many I had to contend with, the second most memorable being when a jumbo pair of shorts I had worn over my swimsuit slipped in my last lap in the pool, causing a major commotion among the ladies and gentlemen alike.

I endured the first shivers of winter with a thermos filled with hot coffee to gulp down between swim sets. In 2006, I had moved into a high-rise with a swimming pool and had a neighbour complain to a watchman when I wore a wetsuit to swim in during the winters. The neighbour was afraid I was polluting the pool. Funnily enough, I had never seen him use the pool to begin with. His kids had a separate pool to swim in, and the one time that he did come down to swim in his shorts, he just lounged by the pool wall, beadily watching my every move. I suppose it was creepy, but I focused on keeping my eyes shut and stayed away from him and his overly buoyant shorts.

I took to running nearly all of the Indian road races at the time, because I really wanted to compete as often as possible. Travelling overseas was a huge financial burden. After my first Ironman attempt, one of my first races in India was the Hyderabad Half-Marathon. Race morning was very relaxed. We got to the start line and stood around until the gun went off. I quickly worked myself to the front and saw the lead pack of women ahead of me. I thought it would be a good exercise to try and keep them in sight for as long as I could. Ten minutes later, a girl in a navy-blue track suit ran up alongside me and asked, 'Has the race started?' I smiled and looked over to see if she was making a joke, but she was dead serious, almost stressed. I said, 'Yes, it has.' She took off instantly, like a bat out of hell. That was a rather humbling moment for me, but I could not stop grinning. I had just noticed that she had no shoes on and her long plait was swaying left and right. A few men exclaimed loudly as she passed them, and I had to laugh out loud. These were the sheroes of Indian running.

I came up to those men within the first 10 km and realized that they were from the army. Having trained with the Madras Sappers once, I thought they would be a fun group to run with, but they were not interested in fun. Within 3 km it became abundantly clear that they were pacing off me. I got pissed. This was an open race, without pace bunnies, without costumes. Added to the nuisance and heavy breathing on my shoulder, the group was too close for comfort. I pulled away from them, even though I was running pretty hard to begin with, and managed to lose them in a few kilometers. I ran well under an hour and fifty minutes and placed ninth overall, surprising myself.

At the finish line, I was completely dehydrated and my calves were cramping severely. I had to lie down, cursing silently. I was mad at myself for not asking the girl her name and mad at the men who had paced off me, making me forget to drink any water throughout. In short, I was mad at everything all at once. I stopped cursing only when I saw a sagely man walking over to check on me. It was Gopichand, the legendary badminton coach from Hyderabad. He was surprisingly genuine in person. Later, I found out that he was a man of strong principles, and had turned down lucrative sponsorships from big soft-drink companies. I also had delusions once about being offered a job at a cola company, but given that high-fructose, corn-syrup and processed cereals are not on my list of nutritional items, I am glad I had Gopichand to look up to. Like him, I would rather endorse that elusive thing called free will.

As I walked towards the stage where they were giving away the awards, I ran into Mrs Leelamma Alaphonso a gem in Indian distance-running, for the first time. She looked very much like the girl who had run up to me in no shoes. She was fit, dressed in a navy-blue track suit and had this huge, incandescent smile. She slapped me on the back and said, 'Achcha kiya!' I nodded and smiled, suddenly struck dumb. I was experiencing my first girl-crush. I wanted to say something super-intelligent, which would make her remember me forever, become my friend, and share training stories with me. Nothing came out of my mouth, though. It was utterly dry. I coughed, ran to get a small bottle of water, and gathered my wits to say a few full sentences to her. I introduced myself and said I was from Bangalore. She said she was from Bombay and had two daughters. I said I knew that, and I was familiar with all her records, too. She smiled even wider and said that not many people were. I asked about her health – I knew that she had suffered a major injury not so long ago – and she said she was feeling better. She still ran sub 3.30 marathons after recovering from a fractured femur.

My inheritance as an Indian endurance athlete comes from women like her, with their bright smiles. These women epitomize an undeniable optimism that is infectious. We only had a brief conversation before we had to go up on stage to collect our prize. I was a bit embarrassed to be collecting any prize, the lead pack had been ahead of me by twenty to thirty minutes. Once I got on stage though, I felt happy. There was not a huge audience, just some random people I had never met, sharing the stage with me and a few photographers. I did my bit and ran down to continue talking to Leelamma. We did not have a very long conversation. She had to go and I had to get in the car to head back home to work on Monday. But I ran into her consistently after that – she always knew the right thing to say and she had great advice to offer on survival. I never had any heroes, but I count her amongst the people I really admire. I was happy that we got to commiserate for a while and her smile made me buy a year's supply of dental floss – my vampire-like canine teeth, not helped by the lack of braces as a young girl, and general change of perspective made me realize that it was very important to smile at the odds.

Even though I placed with the elites in the early races and was often the best amateur, I did not for a second think that I could skip the training or the work that my own sport, triathlon, entailed. I was in awe of the elite women because they showed me the value of truly loving something beyond expectations of glory or money. In my second edition at the Hyderabad Half, I placed one position higher.

I sometimes wonder what sustained sponsorship and some added attention might have done for the legacy of Indian running. We have Bollywood hoo-haas with big-ticket endorsements for products, whose quality the stars are not responsible for. How many face creams and new fashion statements can one be expected to try in a calendar year? In contrast, we have the icons of running, retiring at forty to relative obscurity. I was eager to find out what made someone like Leelamma tick, as a person, as a mother and as an athlete. Sport for me was never about the fame or the spotlight as much as it was about the thrill of adventure, the hours of toil and the simple joy of deep sleep. I found myself in a very new place after my early races. I learned to smile through my discomfort, which was really my cultural inheritance from the women distance runners in India – and flossing often helped the photogenic aspect of masking pain.

High on the Himachal Road Transport

Woh jawani jawani nahin
jiski koi kahani na ho
(A youth spent without stories to tell,
is no youth at all)
 —Manjeet Singh, taxi driver, Chandigarh,
 quoting the lyrics of a song from *Kranti*

A few weeks after we returned from Hyderabad, I went on an impulsive trip to Manali. The first leg of the journey to the mountains was sufficiently comfortable, with a direct flight to New Delhi from Bangalore. The next part was a sixteen-hour ride in a crowded bus, with a lot of different people. Himachal Road Transport seemed determined to shake the last bit of fear out of my gut. I was sure the bus was going to tip over at any moment into a seemingly bottomless gorge. Added to this was everyone's curiosity about me, this woman who dared to travel alone. I felt naked. Luckily for me, I found companionship part of the way with another lone traveller, who looked like she was running away from something. I asked myself whether I was too. What was I hoping to find? Acceptance? The hope of being able to reset my life here? What exactly I was after, I had no clue. I spent the night on the last few seats, spread out comfortably, but insanely paranoid that the chap in the seat ahead of me was more interested in groping me than getting some sleep. It was total rubbish, of course. The man was asleep in no time, but the paranoia was well founded. I woke up to the shadow of his face two inches from mine. That's the way the seats were built. But the guy turned out to be pretty polite and decent, as I discovered when the bus broke down for two hours at 5 a.m. I also discovered a friend in three-year-old Ashmit, who broke into a run at the slightest challenge and drank my tea when we stopped for refreshments. We exchanged views on everything, from teachers to rhymes to tea. I lied about where I was from, to most people. I lied, saying that I was going to meet old friends. I was a total wimp, scared out of my wits once I realized that travelling alone was not too smart. Not on Himachal Road Transport, at least.

After travelling nearly twenty-four hours from Bangalore, when we finally got to Manali, my heart was in a quiet bind at the unspeakable beauty of the place. It's like the grasp of that one, true love. I felt as if the mountains were saying those seven magic words: *I will always be there for you.* There were times when I wondered how I would find meaning in my existence after those closest to me were no more, but this offered new promise.

After travelling nearly twenty-four hours from Bangalore, I called a bike guide whom I spoke to for exactly seven minutes. I wanted to know where I could ride my bike. It was easy to fall in love all over again with my bike and the vertical challenges thereof. I used to think I had a raw deal as a woman engineer. Nonsense! My road thus far had been easy.

The first day in Manali was uneventful. I rented a bike, got introduced to the trails by the bike guide I had talked to on the phone, and was on my way. I had to trust this guy for a few hours of riding, so I used the age-old lie of the boyfriend who didn't exist, who was a Mitochondrial genius and played the guitar for me. The guide, who had been getting the wrong idea until then, backed off after that. I concluded that *The Hitchhikers Guide to the Galaxy*, when written with a feminist perspective, should include a boyfriend, or at least a good story thereof, as an incredibly valuable commodity to carry, besides a toothbrush and a towel, on long journeys.

The next day, I woke up and rode for a few hours at 2,500 feet amdist breathtaking scenery. It was difficult to put words to it. Everything shimmered – from the beautiful kids who thought I was a foreigner because I wore a helmet, to the locals who responded to my loud namastes, to the bus with two dozen school children and a sodding drunk by the side of the road, to the screaming descents where I was clutching my brakes for dear life, to the beautiful trees, the fresh, cool, forgiving air and the clouds that covered the mountains, draping them in a protective embrace as if to say *get closer, get closer, you'll get a hug too*. As we rode through small villages, the kids yelled, 'Kahan ja rahe ho, madam?' and I yelled back, 'Pata nahin!'

I was a little conflicted in my mind about riding my bike past these villages, where basic sustenance seemed to be a struggle. I was conflicted about having spent so much money to travel to Manali, to ride my bike. It occurred to me that the locals seemed to be walking everywhere. I wondered if the local women there rode their bikes for fun. I felt some guilt in being there, it felt hedonistic, but the feeling soon vanished in my efforts to keep the amorous bike guide at bay and just ride to my heart's content.

In the months leading up to my departure from Madison, I used to daydream that I was standing at the very top of a gorgeous emerald mountain, barefoot. I wore green pants rolled up at the ankles, my father's old shirt, my face was covered in dirt and my bike helmet was in my hand, at the end of a long day's work. From where I was standing I could see for miles, but no one could see me. In my dream I was singing, to all my failures and successes. For me, prayer was two parts song, one part endeavour and one part faith. Now, in Manali, I asked myself whether this was my emerald mountain.

The ride was successful. We rambled back into town, talking about environmental issues, when I noticed my soulmate, the river Beas, frolicking like an unaffected spirit. If a river is defined by its shores, its water, and the music that emanates from it, this was certainly the happiest river I had ever met. Later that night, I met six new people, all cyclists from various parts of the world. We swapped stories of training, non-profits and jazz and ate some very tasty food by the river, watching the rain come down.

The day after that was my last day there. The rain had not stopped
since the previous night. After running for an hour, I took a bus back
to Delhi. When I discovered that I had paid Rs 300 more than some
other passengers for the bus ticket, I was angry. I asked the driver, 'Yeh
kyaa baat hai?' to which he responded, 'Duniya mein kya nahin hota
madam?' I wanted to laugh but I had to maintain the impression that
I was raging. I kicked up a fuss and swapped seats with a guy who had
moved to the driver's cabin to help him with alternative routes, since
the one we were supposed to take was waterlogged.

The bus had to climb a mountain and cross a bridge to get to the
other side. My life flashed before my eyes again. We stopped for an hour-
and-a-half because of a landslide ahead. In the meantime, I realized I
had been a jerk to the guy whose seat I had taken without warning
and I apologized to him, mentioning that I had been overcharged and
did not like being taken for a ride. He and his buddy turned out to
be really nice people; Ravi and Ravi. They were great friends, making
plans, swapping stories, and talking to a little kid who was speaking a
mile a minute in Bengali in the seat behind them. A couple of foreign
tourists were travelling with us. I consider myself a stubborn camper,
but the bathroom breaks on this trip were the pinnacle of character
building. The bus driver who charged me extra ended up paying Rs
1,500 to a corrupt cop the next morning, so who was taking whom for
a ride and why?

Brazilian Brouhaha

Buon giorno, Principessa!
—*Life is Beautiful*, Guido

Training in Bangalore was going well until one day in 2007, when I was out riding my bike early in the morning and realized that two men were following me on a moped. This continued for nearly twenty minutes. They were spouting profanities, thinking perhaps that I did not understand Hindi. I understood it only too well. I quickly made my way to the most crowded spot on my route, which shortly after 5 a.m. was a bus-stop right after R.V. College. Every morning, labourers packed up, got on a bus, and came into Bangalore from Mandya. I got on the bus, explained to the driver that I needed my bike to be loaded on the top and he obliged, as he could see I was in trouble. I thought it was a one-off incident, but those two men found me again within a week, when I was almost finishing a three-hour ride. I knew my routes had become predictable. Thankfully, I noticed them quicker the second time around and boarded a bus from a different stop. This time, the driver was not so friendly and cursed at me until one lady with a basket laden with fruit shouted right back at him. I was so grateful to her that I was almost in tears.

I turned to my father for advice. He simply said, 'Go to Madras and ride there on the weekends. You can stay with Periamma. Be honest with her about where you are going. I know a driver, he can help you.' This was just one of the several times that my father would stun me with his vast – and vastly understated – support of my dreams. My father is as tough as nails, but full of heart. You have to earn it with him, though. There's no free lunch with Appa. No pampering. No false encouragement or silent betting on our failure or forcing his kids to live life his way. He has supported every decision my brother and I have made in our lives, even if it was not the best decision, because he believes that it's our life.

I started commuting to Madras on the weekends to ride my bike. I would pack up and leave Bangalore on Friday, train in Madras all weekend, and return to Bangalore on Monday morning. The Madras Mail became a close friend. I made friends with a driver whom my father knew. He introduced me to a quick route to get on the highway between Madras and Pondicherry. The East Coast Road was epic and very seldom moody. At the time, it was not dotted with as much construction as it is today, and it was free riding for a hundred miles, without any stops. It was also unbelievably hot. I would wake up around 3.30 a.m. and feel a light layer of sweat form, even before starting to exercise. My clothes would pretty much be stuck on me, from beginning to end. I felt a great kinship with the unsung gods of cotton clothes and covered legs on these rides in the Indian summer. The humidity also meant I was careful to replenish my body with fluids.

Madras worked 50 per cent harder than Bangalore, any day of the week. I could get a steaming cup of coffee at 4 a.m., without any difficulty. I used to frequent a little tea shop at the start of my ride, often admiring the cook, who would be chopping up at least five kilos of onions faster than Julia Child, while getting my beverage of choice ready. I was never followed, and on longer rides I had the driver hop points on the highway for me, where he would follow me till a certain point, wait for an hour, have a cup of coffee, read a newspaper, and find me ahead on the road, just in case. Most mornings I was done by 9 a.m., so I could get home, eat at my favourite joint, Saravana Bhavan, and read a book. In the evenings, I would go to IIT Madras, which was located on several acres of fenced, forested land. To get past the gates, I often made up a story about visiting one of my two friends who were teaching there, and ran for several hours, undisturbed. What I loved most about running within that campus was the opportunity to have a silent conversation with my favourite denizens on earth: the trees. I named a few of them along the way, just to keep track of where I was on my run. If my friends were actually in town and I found them at home, I would shower and eat at their place and crash if I was too tired. The weekends were the happiest days of my week and I really looked forward to them.

It would be several months before the travelling took a toll on me, mostly because of the change in water and weather. I never travelled in the air-conditioned compartments on the trains because my body could not adapt, even though they were a lot cleaner than the non-air-conditioned ones. I fell sick a lot, especially once the summer started. I was running up to a hundred kilometres a week, while biking as much as I could. Most of my running was indoors: it was safer and smarter.

My second Ironman was in Brazil, in May 2007, and the journey was a lot more interesting. I trained at home all the way up to the race because taxes had to be paid before April. My business was humming and apparently, I forgot that the Ironman was a triathlon, not a duathlon, and consequently forgot to swim for about three months leading up to the race. Traffic in Bangalore was growing by leaps and bounds, in a close race with our projected GDP. I couldn't miss the morning hour, it was both a blessing and a curse. If I slept late on any night (and there were many nights when this happened), I could only close my eyes for a few hours before I had to wake up and run or ride. I did not enjoy this limitation any longer. The adventure was beginning to wear off. The stress was cumulative and for many weeks together, I didn't seem to be able to get beyond thirty-five hours of sleep in a week. I kept telling myself that the positive stories did exist, but I just could not recall any of them.

Getting to the start line in Brazil was my greatest challenge and the one promise I made to myself was that if I did start the race and finish the swim, I would tell a few people about my adventures. Flying to the race turned into a nightmare of comic proportions. Getting into JFK, my geographically challenged self was looking forward to the

short hop to South America. When I boarded the TAM Airlines plane,
I remember thinking, 'Wow, this is a massive plane for a short ride.
Damn! It's full!' After passing out for the first three hours, I woke up
in a daze, very confused as to why we had not yet landed. I asked the
air-hostess whether we were flying back to New York. She smiled and
kindly explained that it was a ten-hour flight to Sao Paulo. Apparently,
that was quite a bit further than Mexico. I burst out laughing, waking my
co-passenger. In the midst of all the frustration and stress of preparing
for the race, I had not checked the flight timings.

When we landed in Sao Paulo, I was exhausted. Transiting through
the airport to catch the next flight to Florianopolis, I got a brief glimpse
of the capital city. Two other competitors who had come in with me
from New York were talking about the slums in the city and how they
were some of the biggest in the world. I craned my neck to hear them
because I was surprised. I was not as well-informed as I had thought.
Besides, not knowing the extent of the landmass on which I had landed,
I did not understand the economics of the place. I thought to myself,
'Slums? How can there be an Ironman in the vicinity then?' A short
flight to Florianopolis had us landing on what looked like a honeymoon
island, where even the dirt on the roads seemed to have been freshly
vacuumed. Unlike my outing in Canada, I had saved up for a year to
afford an upscale transfer to my race hotel. A huge air-conditioned bus
picked us up at the airport and took us to the hotel.

In the two days before the race, I ran into a lot of people from
adjoining parts of South America. One group had travelled more than
eighteen hours from Argentina by local transport, probably not unlike
the buses in Himachal Pradesh, to get to the race. My own fancy bus ride
indicated that I was moving up in life but surprisingly, I did not enjoy
the thought. I preferred wearing second-hand clothes, negotiating with
cows in Bangalore, struggling with rude cab drivers and assembling
my own bike in a cheap hostel. It was the mental training that made
me stronger. I realized then that my relationship with money would
always be a complicated one. I would always want to make enough to
pay my bills, travel a little and never depend on anyone. I did not need

After a ride in the Bangalore monsoon, 2005

Running alongside Bangalore traffic and laughing at people's comments, 2005

Hyderabad Half-Marathon, 2006, placed ninth

Auckland Half-Ironman, 2006

Amma holding her newborn in New Delhi, 1980, and Amma holding her not-so-newborn in Madurai at the Meenakshi Amman temple, 2012

Amma, Appa and I during my wedding, 2010

My brother and I at the Nalangu ceremony for my wedding, 2010

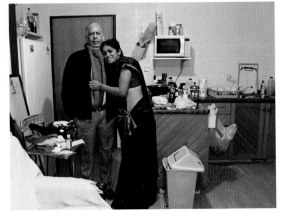

Dad visiting my super-messy studio apartment for my graduation, May 2010

With my advisor
Mark Billinghurst
after the graduation
ceremony, 2010

Defending my PhD
thesis, 2010

Training completed at nearly 1 a.m. during
the time I was writing my thesis, 2009

Riding from Chennai
to Pondicherry, 2007

At the bike transition of
my first-ever Ironman in
Ottawa in fashionable
second-hand flannel
pyjamas, 2006

Running the 70.3 Ironman World
Championship qualification at
Geelong, 2008

With the lovely bike-shop
owner in New Zealand who
helped me buy a bike at
practically no cost, 2008

Backpack on a three-day ride from Christchurch to Nelson, 2009

Wearing the polka-dot jersey in the Five Passes Tour in the Southern Alps of New Zealand, 2009

Riding in the Port Hills in Christchurch, 2010

Three-day ride between Christchurch and Nelson, 2009

At the start of Ultraman Canada with other participants, 2009

At swim practice, 2009

Above and left: Finishing Day 1 and Day 2 at Ultraman Canada with a smile after 270 km, 2009

With the always-inspiring Jason Lester at the start of Ultraman Canada

A ride through California, 2013

Puttin' it down with the legends, Araneta
Coliseum, Philippines, 2010

Walking the Rhine Valley
when 28 weeks pregnant
(somewhere between
Bingen and Koblenz), 2014

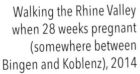

adversity to count my blessings but staying in a dull comfort zone with no impetus to challenge myself was also not my life's goal. I was my parents' daughter first and foremost.

I was put up in a room next to some fast amateur women and some professional athletes. I ran into Brianna again and she was warm and friendly. In these athletes, I saw a strong adherence to regime, but one that was supported by their environment. There was no conflict in their mind about what they wanted to do because everyday training was not a battle. When training in Bangalore, I knew I was struggling with my motivation big time, as evidenced by my lack of swimming. When I complained to Aurora, she simply said, 'To me, your motivation to do what you are doing seems more like a large and often gregarious Phoenix, the mythical bird, not the capital of Arizona.'

Ironman Brazil started and ended at the north-western end of the island with the swim being held at El Divino beach. This ocean swim was one of the many reasons I had picked the race. I was not in the best of minds when the race started, but I was looking forward to my conversation with the waves. I quickly lost my way in the chop of water created by the many competitors ahead of me and had the worst possible swim. The lack of swim training did not help either. Navigating the M-shaped swim course was quite difficult as I was repeatedly boxed in the face by other swimmers. I started the bike ride enraged by the swim and my inability to train well. I was angry about not being able to complete my long rides in Bangalore. I was angry about having to travel to Madras every weekend. I was angry about every city in India that had me waking up at 3:30 a.m. to beat traffic, to ride my bike. Yoda's warning against 'frustration turning into anger' had come true for me after reading in the papers about the CEOs of busy and important corporations in Bangalore publicly debating whether the workforce should be at their desks by 6.30 a.m. Were these companies crazy? When would people exercise, at 8 p.m.? But even in those dark phases, I had not wished for a fancier bike or carbon aerobars or aeroblahs, as I renamed them. I just wanted roads to train on, in my sports bra and shorts if I pleased. An image came to mind, of an argument with my brother over the use of the trusty treadmill. According to him, running for two hours on a treadmill was not good. For the treadmill. I had wanted my little brother to understand that if I had the choice, I would run outside. He didn't, and hence our arguments. I ran at odd hours in training, because the non-glamorous part of a small business was 100 per cent ownership. Yet I continued to train because running was the only way I knew to add some extras in the ordinary. I had more bad days than good ones. I had cranky clients who made me angry. I was unhappy with my training circumstances and felt I was going backwards. Where was my place under the sun?

In Brazil, I took an hour longer than I had in Ottawa on the swim and bike ride. I started the run fuming. For the first time in a long time, I felt like I had something to prove. I ran the marathon in four hours and seven minutes on a course with some inclines. No one passed me on that run. I was determined not to let them, for as long as I could. I placed fifth on the run in my age-group, but the finish was not pretty. The big cloud of despair burst and along with it came a deluge of anger at my lack of training opportunities, always working so hard to go half as fast, having to do so much of the work indoors … it seemed like a winter with no end.

With time, training had become an uphill battle. On the days my commitment did return home, it said, 'Sorry doll, I kinda needed some time to sort through my issues'. We had a bit of a chat and found some new contact lenses to help us see through the traffic on the sweltering roads and trained as much as our circumstances allowed us to. In an attempt to cheer me up, one of my friends remarked, 'You will go down in history as the very first triathlon-nut woman tycoon from India,' and I replied, 'That is a claim to fame as illustrious as the inventors of the first disposable paper cups.'

Once I returned to Bangalore from Brazil, I had some long conversations with my family and some of my friends, and decided to give my PhD another go. One part of me knew that what I really wanted was to train consistently, and living in Bangalore placed limits on my ability to do so. Maybe the sweat from my clothes made the stench of the glass ceiling at Madison disappear from my mind. I went ahead and applied for a PhD programme in New Zealand. I was done with America, academically and professionally. I was pleasantly surprised to get one of the highest paid scholarships from the University of Canterbury, in Christchurch. I decided I would reciprocate the faith my advisor had shown in me with a strong effort in academics, albeit laced with many hours of sport. I left Bangalore thinking, what goes around, comes around. I was determined not to become a customer of disappointment. Luckily for me, I knew I had a tradable commodity – my brain – and I never took it for granted.

NOMADIC LEAP

Aotearoa

It is not the mountain we conquer, but ourselves.
—Sir Edmund Hillary

New Zealand is home to some of the greatest endurance athletes in the world. I had come to understand that since a marathon is not exactly television material, and there isn't enough juice to make it a once-in-four-years-Olympic-frenzy, the tougher endurance sports don't find enough exposure. Rugby, cricket, tennis, football and badminton are the sports that get regular coverage to an absurd degree. Kiwis, however, have a hardy attitude when it comes to sidestepping the politics involved in sport and focusing on what they love. This made me put my own troubles in perspective.

Once I got to New Zealand in September 2007, I quickly got into a routine. There were enough factors for motivation: the traffic-free roads, the clean swimming pools, and a scholarship to pay my bills. I swam to my heart's content at the QE2, the local Olympic-sized pool with 50-metre lanes, all drawn lengthwise. I also joined groups of athletes who swam at Sumner beach and other open-water bodies over the weekends. The water in New Zealand was clear blue and sometimes jade green. It was cold for the most part, but stunning to swim in. I ran in Bottle Lake Forest, the New Brighton beach, or the hills in the Banks Peninsula. The Bottle Lake Forest had mostly pine trees and several run-loops, including the Blue Loop, which was my staple. As opposed to Umstead State Park in North Carolina, the Arboretum in Madison and the fenced forests at IIT Madras, the ground in Bottle Lake was as beautiful as the trees themselves, lined with mosses, many types of ferns, and mushrooms when it was wetter. Running through this forest was like gliding effortlessly on a smooth carpet. New Brighton beach had several dunes and it was not always flat running. I preferred running at high-tide because it meant less human traffic and the crashing of waves was mysteriously soothing.

Riding in Christchurch and the surrounding areas was a dream compared to Bangalore. I biked to university, 17 km one way. Most of the highways were accessible within twenty minutes of riding out of the city. My favourite loops were in the hills, up Evans Pass or Dyers Pass, onto the roads that led into Lyttleton Harbor and then into Sumner and back out to the city. Another favourite ride was to Akaroa, a 180-km round trip with 3,500 metre elevation gain. There was a great ice-cream shop at Akaroa, which made the effort well worth it. All these places were parts of the Banks Peninsula, named after Joseph Banks, Captain Cook's botanist on the *HMS Endeavour*. The peninsula itself had been formed after a volcanic eruption.

I also ran up in the hills, quite a lot. Some of my favourite workouts included riding up Dyers Pass, from the town of Cashmere in Christchurch. I would park my bike at a local coffee shop and run for several hours through podocarp forests, at the top of the hills. I never needed the aid of music on these runs. There were plenty of songbirds, including the beautiful blackbird, thrushes and finches. The undergrowth was filled with weird grasses and the runs went past several farms and sheep grates. It was as if I were running straight into the arms of the blue sky, which was visible for miles above the hills. I asked myself whether this was the emerald mountain from my dream, and not the one in Manali, and felt lucky to arrive at my dream's destination more than once in life.

The road between Christchurch and Hanmer Springs was mostly flat, for a good 140–160 km one way, depending on the starting point in Christchurch. The rides in and around Christchurch varied in terrain and I had a lot to pick from. I sought out groups to ride with, dressed in all the wrong clothes as usual, and typically lost the group within 5-10 minutes of setting out – apparently my VO2-max had a foreign quality to it. I loved being at the back of the pack when I started training in a group – it gave me a goal to work towards. Then I got to the middle of the group, then even further ahead than that.

Within a few months of consistent training, I set out on a ride on a route I had taken on my first visit to New Zealand in 2006. It looped up one big climb, about 17 km into the ride. The climb itself was along Dyers Pass, which was about 5 km long. That morning had been challenging, with a rude Kiwi swim coach getting on my case about some India-New Zealand cricket match and following that up with a question about mail-order brides from India. This coach had tried getting under my skin from the very first day I showed up at his squad with a towel around my waist. I felt weird showing up in a swimsuit, even in New Zealand. After many months of trying to break me, using many different names he came up with – the one that made me laugh the most was 'Here comes the world's fastest Indian' – he realized that I was not one to take myself too seriously.

Anyway, I was fuming by the time the swim was over, but my angst worked in my favour that day. A little coffee and ten doses of the prescribed portion of peanut-butter for a fat-free life helped me make the decision to try the loop, which seemed pretty intimidating. You could lose your soul up in the hills around Christchurch because, in stark contrast to Bangalore, you literally don't see a human being for miles out there. The climb was surprisingly easy and I was done in thirty-three minutes. Local champions were doing the loop in about twenty-five minutes, so I was thrilled. The second part of the loop went through some rollers on the leeward side of the hills into Lyttleton Harbor. I was flying on this section, which came to an end quicker than I had expected. I started wondering then if I had lost my way or missed a turn. Except, of course, missing a turn would have meant diving head-first off the sheer face of the cliffs I was riding along.

Two-and-a-half hours into the ride, rain started to patter down, but thanks to the peanut-butter, I was quite ensconced. I wasn't even nervous about my brakes, which seemed a bit slippery. Before I knew it, I was in the last part of the loop that travels out and yonder into Sumner, over what looks like an elephant's head. This elephant did not believe in manicures and had several emerald patches of pine trees surrounding its fingertips, as though it had just got done chopping up a bunch of mushrooms and the mud from the mushrooms had collected on its fingertips. I found it hard to contain my excitement because the clock seemed unmoving. The final part of the ride was a 2-km descent on Evans Pass and then a 19-km flat section back to Christchurch. I was home in about 4 hours 7 minutes. I looked up my log and found that I had gained about fifty minutes within twenty-one months. Same loop, same girl, a slightly better attitude and hairstyle to boot!

The day after that ride, there was a big hailstorm. I was tired after my long day out in the boonies. I had started to cautiously date a tall, soft-spoken German boy in Christchurch. He was extremely curious about how I balanced sport and work and while he never pretended to understand all of it, he was generous and kind with his time. The day of the hailstorm, however, we had an argument because he did not understand why a ride was so much more exciting than a movie. Miffed with his lack of understanding, I took off on a long run.

A few months later, in November 2007, I participated in a Half Ironman held in Ashburton. The race directors had chosen a stellar swim venue at Lake Hood. Ashburton is literally in the middle of nowhere. The terrain is mostly flat, the water clean, and the race promised to be boring. It started the Kiwi way, in an atmosphere that was slack and relaxed. Most competitors were focused on their preparations, some of them in hot-pink speedos. Triathletes are really snazzy dressers, if nothing else. The combination of loud swim togs and compression socks was enough to make me giggle. I remember thinking there could be no better start to the day than jumping in a lake and romancing some underwater chlorophyll.

I was out in forty-one minutes after a two-loop swim. About 100 of us then ran out to our bikes and biked around a flat, three-loop course. The weather was perfect. I was hoping it would get really hot just in time for the run. During my training for Ironman Brazil in Madras, I had come to discover that one of my alter egos was the humble water buffalo. I loved the heat. Better still, I loved the prospect of being half-soaked in water, while the air temperatures were searing the top of my head. We were a match made in heaven, the water buffalo and I. Additionally, water buffaloes believe in the economy of words. They are truly the genius cousins of the holy cows who kept me company on my many rides in India. I was the genius cousin of the many unholy choices I seemed to be making, pursuing sport and attempting to get a PhD.

My prospects in Ashburton were looking grim, though. Those Kiwis could really bike! They may or may not be aerodynamic, but any ninety-year-old Kiwi could out-pedal me on any given day. Finally, after much prayer and meditation on why staying above average velocity was a much better idea than getting below it, I managed to catch one competitor on the bike. I even did the Lance Armstrong, look-back-and-show-'em-how-strong-I-am neck-twist. It took me 3 hours and 27 minutes to finish the bike ride and I felt fantastic.

The run is my favourite part and by the time I started it, everyone else was ahead of me, except the one person I had passed. Just the night before, I had been reading about Emil Zatopek, a legendary runner called 'the locomotive', who grunted loudly as he ran, his head bouncing from side to side, an image of pain and suffering. Since I imagined that my overall struggle-fest on the run made me look like him, I had a conversation in my head with my long-dead, maybe-hero.

Emil Zatopek, in a voice like Denzel Washington's: 'I was a good runner, Anu. You may think you look like me, but you are just the friendly neighbourhood walrus who wheezes.'

Me: 'Running? Please! Try a tri-sometime. Besides, I am a water buffalo, not a wheezing walrus. Dude, you ever BEEN to India? Get your fauna right!'

Emil : 'Why you gotta have this attitood? You are a walrus, plain and simple.'

Me: 'Water buffalo.'

Emil: 'Walrus. Why you shouting? The pace too much for ya?'

Me, now panting: 'Water ... bu ... ffa ... lo.'

I pushed him out of my head and ate a Mars bar to drown my sorrows. It was the first race in New Zealand where people actually knew me by name. So every time someone said, 'Go Anu!' I would pick up the pace. On the last lap of the three-lap run, the temperatures were right where I wanted them and the final shout of 'Hey Anu! Your Heineken is waiting!' got me across the finish line in an hour and fifty-seven minutes. I did pretty well on the race, placed eighth overall, and was pleased with my progress.

A fortnight or so later came a new adventure with the Rotorua Half Ironman, on the North Island. Rotorua was famous for its geysers and mud-baths. A short trip got me and two of my friends from Christchurch, who were also racing, to the Rotorua Regional Airport. When we stepped out of the plane, we were hit by a strong stench of sulphur, which led me to repeat Kristy's joke about the protein shakes we were consuming and how triathletes could fertilize entire forests with their natural emissions. A little sulphur would not kill us.

The swim was held at the Blue Lake or Lake Tikitapu, a really happy, deep lake that must have been Buddhist in its past life. This was one of the smaller lakes in the Bay of Plenty, but it seemed metaphorical in its abundance. It was not man-made, so I figured I stood a chance. A year ago, I could not have imagined racing twice, just a few weeks apart, let alone racing two triathlons in quick succession. But I was itching to go that morning. Treading water, I was caught between the darkest depths of my soul and the sheer immensity of living in the moment. I found myself wistfully desiring a long, difficult day with the gods of weak quads. On the swim I found that the pack had left me within five minutes. A second later, I realized that I was the pack. At the 900-metre mark on the swim, I was sure that life was a total and complete blast. I exited the water in forty-three minutes.

The bike ride in Rotorua was over some major climbs. *One step for elite athletes, a giant leap for an Indian walrus.* Damn Emil, he was back in my head. I decided to take the bike course piece by piece. A really nice lady and I got into a little game of sorts, passing and re-passing each other, which made the time go by fast. After getting through 83 km in less than three hours at a speed of nearly 28 kph, the last 7 km took twenty-three minutes, dropping my pace to 18 kph. While tackling the last few climbs, I switched to the granny gear on my bike, half wishing I had never been born.

The run was partly in the bush and then some nice little loops. I had no idea where I was for the most part. Delirium was getting the better of the Mars bars. Doing two races so close together came with a few consequences. The proverbial piano was about to fall when the run course took us through some killer stairs. After some ups and downs, I did make it to the finish line, having run the half-marathon in two hours. I was dished out some major humility at that race. True to its billing, at the Rotorua Half Ironman, the pain was never far away. After the race, we took a little trip to the hot pools. Sitting in one, I thought to myself that I was a few light-years away from greatness and I was losing weight in the process. So it was a win-win situation. I placed in the top three on the run, on a hilly course. That was my paycheck for the day.

On Winning

The will to win is not nearly so important as the will to prepare to win.

—Vince Lombardi

When I think about the global obsession with winning, I often think about Jerry Seinfeld's quote in response to the merits of watching the New York City Marathon: 'Ah, what's to see? A woman from Norway, a guy from Kenya and 20,000 losers.' In terms of absolute wins, it's tough to argue that Seinfeld is incorrect. I did not report my results in Indian races or blog about anything for the first three years. I never thought about money as part of the equation. I knew for a fact that for at least five years into the game, there would be no significant sponsorship to speak of, and I did not look for it. The times I really wished for financial support, I circled back to the knowledge that some things just don't have a price tag.

It was nearing Christmas in 2007 and to us gleeful residents of the southern hemisphere, it seemed that the weather could not have been more perfect. A few of us who swam together were debating whether to join a bigger group that was putting together a training camp. Most of us were in the process of training for a Half Ironman at Geelong and an Ironman in New Zealand. I was still working around ten to twelve hours a week on my business in Bangalore from New Zealand via calls and emails. My weekly schedule was unrelenting. I was in the pool by 6 a.m., at work by 9.30 a.m., trained at lunch, and then again in the evening, starting at 6. On the days when I had only two workouts, I called in to my office in Bangalore. There were many weeks when my PhD, sport and office demanded more than ninety hours in my weekly schedule. During one of these, I considered an offer made by a third party, to buy a portion of our business, by investing some money in return. The thought had never crossed my mind before, but with increasing work pressure, and the need to hire more people, I felt I should consider the offer. I was to speak to the businessman who had initiated contact, but I put it off for a fortnight to gather my thoughts.

I had been feeling a little lost that Thursday, questioning my own motivations in taking on all of my overwhelming pursuits. People partake in sports in many different ways. Was I making things harder for myself by doing a PhD and sport together? There was no alternative in my mind. I felt more stranded than lost. New Zealand was a small island. After living in India and the continental United States, it seemed smaller to me, in more ways than one. The people were the clincher, though. Kiwis were hardy, humble, and had better attitudes compared to what one finds in India and in the United States. The camp I was about to head to offered perspective on the company I kept and the reason I loved keeping that company.

To take a vacation from my worries, I decided to take Friday off and attend the training camp organized by the local tri-club. On reaching the pool from where we were scheduled to depart, I realized that I had grossly underpacked. I had one water bottle, one energy bar, two bars of chocolate, and that was it. I did not have any spare tyres, a second and third bottle, or matching gear, like 70 per cent of the campers did. I grabbed a Powerade from the vending machine, stuck it in my jersey, and set out with the rest of them.

We started riding from the pool with a small backpack stuffed with some clothes for the weekend. I started out with a slower group, which left earlier than the rest. I preferred an early start on most days. The pace was social for the first 20 km from Christchurch to Kaiapoi, after which I got a tad impatient and took off in the front. Riding in a group is a little tricky; it's political and requires etiquette, which fails me ever so often. For instance, while riding in a group, you keep your front wheel in close proximity to the back wheel of the rider ahead of you, to achieve an aerodynamic advantage. In a triathlon, it is illegal to draft off the wheel of the rider in front of you, but that is precisely what one is expected to do in a group ride. Since I had packed neither my measuring tape nor my patience that day, I soon found myself in the front, riding solo. Within 50 km, the group caught up with me and went ahead. Although I didn't think anything of it, apparently my little stunt of pulling ahead did not go down well. I still didn't care. I ate my chocolate and hung onto the wheel of the last rider, just to regain my senses. Suddenly, I heard a shriek from upfront. Looking up from my aerobars, I could see arms flailing, hand pumps being wielded like daggers of Megiddo from the old horror movie *The Omen*, the group going helter-skelter, and definitely no pace line being maintained. Magpies! Magpies are commonly found in Australia and New Zealand. During their breeding season, most bikers find themselves subjected to the occasional dive bomb from the treetops, the birds' response to any perceived threats. A number of contraptions, including zip ties on helmets, had been suggested to me, but I was not prepared. Luckily, the more experienced Kiwis upfront fielded most of the attacks, with no casualties. However, it was enough to rattle the group and we pulled over for a quick pit stop shortly thereafter. Some friendly trash talk followed, after which I took off with a smaller set of people, with headphones on and not a care in the world about magpies or other avalanches from the heavens above. When we got into Hanmer Springs 140 km later, I was reminded of my soulmate – the river Beas. The entrance into Hanmer takes you over a one-way bridge across a river with a spectacular view of the Southern Alps, which start to appear closer from that point on the road. While the river in Hanmer did not have the velocity or the sheer force of will that the Beas does, it still made me cry. I found myself sniffling like an idiot for a full five minutes.

At the intersection of a ski lodge and the forest, I waited for the rest of my group to catch up. Once they did, I was sure I was going in the right direction, towards our accommodation for the weekend. An hour of running after that ride helped us locate the Waterfall Track, and the time passed quite easily, surrounded by pine and spruce forests, alpine air, and athletic company. We were close to the Hanmer Forest, which was spread over 30,000 acres.

Then came the weekend-long crush on a guy whose name was Drew-something, who seemed to be an Irish Yoga teacher with a Canadian passport and a Scottish accent. I was still dating my German engineer, but I was very impressed with Drew's friendly manner and larger-than-life love for his bike. This character rolled in as I was swapping stories with three boys: Tim, Herbert and Colt. We were laughing about the time when Dave, about 100 km into the ride, came riding up from the opposite direction shouting, 'Are there people behind you?' in a Kiwi accent I did not understand. I had immediately jumped to the conclusion in my sugar-depleted state that he was a mass murderer, and pedalled insanely fast into Hanmer.

As it turned out, Adam, code-named Shrek, had a lover. I was totally depressed on Saturday morning when I woke up and found him lying in her arms. To get over my romantic bedlam, I went on a run in the adjoining forest, towards the Waterfall Track, in my pyjamas. I ran about 7.5 km in forty minutes or so on gravel paths, without my Walkman for company, surrounded by mountains that looked like frozen chocolate, and promptly forgot about my man troubles. I also forgot about the morning group swim and went in a good half hour late. We were swimming in a heated, outdoor pool, but the ambient temperatures were still pretty crisp in the morning. It was cold when my arms came out of the water on a stroke and warm when I put them back in. Cold, hot, cold, hot. Like eating raisins and pretzels from one bowl. Sweet, salty, sweet, salty.

Shrek had followed me into the pool and was swimming in the lane next to me. Unrequited love, especially in a girl more used to love handles than love notes, usually turns to anger quite quickly. When Shrek said something like, 'I see we are staying for the next set too, eh?' it was enough to piss me off. I wondered if he was showing off, besides looking totally adorable. While I had a huge urge to pinch his bottom, I was temporarily distracted by Drew, Shrek's best friend, in his hot pink speedos. After swimming for nearly an hour-and-a-half, I got out of the pool and headed back to my room. That afternoon, we had bike-run reps scheduled, to practise transitions. It sounded a bit over the top to me, but in the spirit of being social, I started with the group. Some of the group I had ditched in the last segment of our ride the previous day were not over my lack of group etiquette, and were intent on teaching me a lesson. One lady in particular kept overtaking me on the run-reps, putting on a surge only when she came up to me on a multiple-loop run. I had to remind myself that I had run once before the swim in the morning. Once again, the ennui of being surrounded by type-A, overly competitive triathletes was setting in. I let her pass me, making no effort to show off, but beginning to wonder when this would end. On the third such rep, in an attempt to cut me off and surge past, she ran straight into a bush on a turn. I stifled my laughter as best as I could, stopped, and waited for her to get up. She didn't take my hand and I thought, 'Oh wow! We are definitely in the camp of prodigies.' When I tried to strike up a conversation later that evening to break the ice, I made no progress. Instead of limiting myself to my age group, I hung out with a couple, Gina and Colt, and heard a lot of great stories.

A third run followed that evening, where I ended up getting lost and logged a few hours of running to the top of the Mount Isobel track, a New Zealand classic. There was sheer faith, and the sweetness of chocolate chips in my mouth on that run, but once again, no music. I was running into what resembled the bush, through more forest, some parts with canopy, some with just dry undergrowth. It was just me, my legs, the thinning air on the climb and the stunning view. I tried to eat more than I required at dinner, causing the lead rider to comment on the size of my plate. But since he was one of the few Kiwis who had been to Madras and was also very good looking, he was given five passes to err.

Over dinner, I discovered that Gina was going to attempt the Five Passes Tour with a slipped disc. The Five Passes Tour was a cycling tour that attracted some of the best amateur athletes on the island. Hard men and women with shiny quads. At the time, I thought it wasn't meant for overweight Indian wannabes like me. I was admittedly a little freaked out, but in awe of the woman's determination.

On Sunday, Shrek, hot-pink-speedo Drew and I woke up at 5 a.m., made some breakfast and set out before 6 a.m. on a ride. It was freezing cold. Ten minutes into the ride, I saw hot-pink-speedo-man return. I shouted out, 'It's friggin' freezing, Mr Bigglesworth,' and he waved back. When I asked what was wrong, he replied, 'You don't wanna know!' I figured he had cracked because it was too cold to be riding. I couldn't feel my toes and none of us had slept well the night before, given the meagre accommodation and sparse heating. Before I knew it though, I had fuelled up on a muffin and coffee and covered 134 km over several hours of riding. I finished the weekend with a cool swim, a jog and some weights.

Late evening on Sunday, I realized that triathlon training is like seeking *The Ring*. We meet all kinds of characters. Some good, some bad, most compulsive, some with a lot of angst, some who have to surge past you at all costs, some who are open-hearted about their aspirations and with a child-like belief that humbles the hardest of sceptics, and others, like me, who are unable to proceed with the expected cultural caution. For me, the best alternative was to limit the damage and make sure that my milestones were marked by great stories.

On Monday, I received a call from the businessman who had offered to invest in my business. Within ten minutes, it became clear to me that he was a fast-talking stockbroker. He launched into a monologue, calling himself a visionary and using big phrases like, 'We like to empower smaller businesses'. He then offered me a position as the CTO of a different company he was funding, knowing fully well that it would be in direct conflict to my own venture. I was so amused by his belligerence that I decided to see where the conversation would lead. He kept babbling a mile a minute about how much money there was to be made, and in the next sub-clause elucidating how money was not the goal, *really*, and how excited he was to be talking to me. When I quizzed him about what he would bring to the table, he said, 'Don't worry, we'll hire the right board to advise you.' Besides money, he didn't seem to be bringing anything to the table. No process discipline. No core competence. I thought the conversation was accelerating downhill even faster than I figured it was. As for his offer of funding my business, the answer clearly was, 'No, thanks!'

There is no textbook answer, is there, to the question of what defines the human spirit? I was a long-course Indian triathlete. That was enough of an oxymoron in itself. That my business would survive storms might seem like an oxymoron too, but I was done feeling bad about it. My business partners and I knew how much sweat and tears went into maintaining independence. Selling out was the last option.

The following week started with a rush to get to work, after a much-needed massage. The massage therapist, as usual, wrapped up the sixty-minute massage in fifty minutes. I pretended to swim after that, but it was only a sorry excuse for a shower. Mondays on my programme involved some fast running and I managed to do what is affectionately called a 3-km time-trial, with each kilometre slower than the one before it. I conveniently missed the adjective 'descending' in my training plan, which required me to speed up and not slow down on my 1,000-metre progressions. To make up for this, I got back into the pool on Tuesday, with some Olympic-swimmer wannabes who were in my lane. This was the lane slower than the slowest lane, where you get to stand up in case you are out of breath in the middle of a lap. I was starting to get a bit peeved with the excessive traffic, but being Indian, I had in-built mechanisms to deal with crowds. That evening, there was a bike time-trial of around 8 km, all uphill, around the Port Hills, where I tacked on some extra hours with a group and rode for close to four hours. On Wednesday, I finished a pretty hard gym session, lifting weights, followed by a ninety-minute run.

And so the week continued, with me averaging some pretty big training numbers. I reminded myself that the Indian-on-an-island syndrome was much more real and fatal compared to the middle-child syndrome. So training a lot was totally warranted. Come Sunday, I had put in my biggest training numbers for the year, and decided to do a little run-race, also in the Port Hills. The Port Hills are probably the best place to run in Christchurch, after the Bottle Lake Forest. The inclines on tracks that go in and out of the hills are great to build strength and I loved training there. To get to the start of the race, I had to bike up Dyers Pass. Halfway there, I had to get off, rehydrate, stop crying, and blow my nose. I was hurting like crazy from the cumulative fatigue of the week's training, totalling over thirty hours.

The Port Hills Summit Road Run was a 20-km hilly run through small, sharp hills. That was only the good news. The better news was that it was around 25 degree Celsius out there. It was *hot*, and my tropical water buffalo alter ego was totally psyched by the time we started. I had no goals for the run, except to survive it. I got a bit carried away and ran the first 5 km in twenty-two and a half minutes. Apparently, Emil's Olympic-runner shadow in the distance influenced me at the start. After this, my pace was pretty even, and I finished in about 103 minutes, behind four forty-plus folk who ran faster than I ever could dream of running. The overall winner, also over forty, finished the race in ninety-two minutes, and I was in fifth. *Not too shabby, I* thought to myself. The week was done and it was time to rest.

With the promise of a book and some green tea, Sunday afternoon seemed vastly appealing to my exhausted senses. I chatted with a few people I knew at the finish of the race and rode back home. Later that night, I found out that I was in a special category in that run race, called the Open Women's category. This pushed the forty-year-olds who beat me into the veteran's category – and it meant that I had won in my category in that race. I shook my head in disbelief and re-loaded the results page ten times to convince myself. Then I biked back to collect my prize(s) – a bottle of New Zealand's finest red, a white towel, some spiffy sunglasses, and a box of tissues. I donated the sunglasses to my mentor and then best friend, blew my nose with my new tissues to see if they worked, stuffed the towel in my back pocket and rode back home. I was proud of my first win at a race.

Showtime in Geelong

Traveller, there are no paths.
Paths are made by walking.
    —an Australian Aboriginal saying

The World Championships for Triathlon were held in North America at both the Ironman and Half Ironman distances, until very recently. The steep entry fee made it not just a great physical challenge, but also a huge expenditure. Some of the top performances in the championships came from competitors hailing from outside North America. Australia and New Zealand had their share of tough competitors, and one of the early races on my calendar was the Half Ironman in Geelong, Australia, in February 2008. This was also meant to serve as a good tune-up for the upcoming Ironman in New Zealand.

Geelong was 80 km away from Melbourne, one of the coolest cities I have been to. In contrast to Bangalore, where all the old landmarks were rapidly disappearing, Melbourne had a sizeable Central Business District, several old but historic buildings, and crazy trams which tried to run everyone down. The trams reminded me of Calcutta, where both hope and the sun rise at 4.30 a.m. and set really late.

It was a quick trip down to Geelong on the Saturday before the race. Life had been going great until that point. I had been training consistently and knew that I was where I wanted to be with my milestones. I reminded myself that I had not been swimming at all in the lead-up to Ironman Brazil, but had finished it just fine.

I warmed up by running on the beach before the start of the race and felt fit, ready and positive. We had a deep-water start and I told myself that no matter what, I was going to finish the swim strong. We had been warned on race morning of sea-urchins, and that was playing on my mind a little, as I had no idea what sea-urchins were. Were they baby jellyfish, or humanoid furry beasts with flaring nostrils, or cantankerous mini-whales? Who knew? My undersea scan did not bring up anything resembling any of these, only a lot of seaweed. The sun was in our face nearly the whole time, until the swim turnaround, and that made things interesting. After the turnaround, I got a little bored with the overrated urchin-scare and swam hard to the finish. I exited the water in forty-four minutes, slower than I had anticipated. But I didn't care.

My goals for the race were to minimize transition time and bike my guts out. A Canadian named Tara Norton was out there on the course somewhere. Tara and I had met briefly in Christchurch. She had survived a major accident and worked her way out of the hospital to several podium finishes with killer consistency. I loved that lady! She was so strong and determined that she made everyone else look boring. By the time I huffed and puffed through the second lap of the bike-course, Tara had caught up. She said, 'Go Anu!' and I immediately had a vision in which I was being labelled the next lean, mean cycling machine. I mean, if Tara Norton had just said 'Go Anu!' and Tara Norton had taught all the silly boys a lesson on the bike, it clearly meant I had potential. Off I went, to make the last lap the fastest of the three. I was done with my bike ride in 3 hours and 26 minutes, including the swim transition.

The transition to the run was also accomplished in record time, so I had every reason to smile. The lead women were exceptional runners. The run itself was a clinical affair, but it felt like a lot of physical and mental factors came together for me, for the first time in a long time. I was working pretty hard and I kept thinking positive thoughts. I thought about my crazy friends, the way they had conquered their bad attitudes. I thought about Tara Norton, who was also running to her finish when I set out, looking like a million bucks and delivering great results. I thought about my nemesis, a competitor in my category, who was ten seconds ahead of me. I thought about the Mars bars and how I needed to get a better nutrition plan, as the sweet taste was getting icky. I thought about my feet and how much they were going to enjoy the rest and downtime. I thought about the German boy in my life. Sure, he did not run or bike or swim, but he was very, very smart and surely, I didn't want to date a replica of myself, did I? I thought about my mother and father, who are my blue sky in any given race. I thought about my brother, who had just run a sub-two hour half-marathon.

At the end of all that thinking, I sailed through to the finish line with a 1:49 run, the highlight of my day, finishing the Half Ironman in 6 hours and 57 seconds. I had missed the six-hour mark by fifty-seven seconds, but I would find out later that evening, at the post-race awards party, that I had qualified for the Half Ironman 70.3 World Championships in Florida. My hopes had not been misplaced after all.

On my flight back to Christchurch, I did the math and realized that I would not be able to afford to get to Florida later in the year. Also, it would be summer in New Zealand, and I would not want to miss that. Besides, it was five months since I had started my PhD, and my academic work had just sputtered to life after a paper that my advisor and I submitted had been accepted at a conference. It was a position paper, discussing the data-sets we intended to use in our study, and it was a small conference, but it would be a meaningful milestone in my research. The lab I was working in had good facilities and, most importantly, a multi-disciplinary pool of students. There were engineers, designers and artists. I felt more at home in that lab than anywhere else, academically.

As I watched Australia disappear, I closed my eyes with a smile on my face. I did not care that I could not make it to the World Championships. I had plenty of work staring me in the face. I had to call Bangalore to tell my parents what I had just achieved. I had to meet the boy I was dating and finally spend two hours with him at a stretch.

I had to work on the paper that was to be published. I had to get back on the run track, in the glorious February summer. The good news was that there were toilets I could use at the new track, there was no need to go looking for five-star hotels. There were about three weeks left to Ironman New Zealand. I had to hustle.

Lyrical Lydiard

It's a lot of hard work for five, six or seven years.
There's no secret formula.
There's no shortcut to the top.
                                            —Arthur Lydiard

Arriving in Taupo for Ironman New Zealand three weeks later, I
was in a spot of trouble with my back. I had pulled one long week
at work, and the sitting probably affected my muscles. I had stepped up
the swimming to compensate for the lack of time on my bike. Still, I was
happy to be in Taupo. I felt lucky and eager to do my very best.

Lake Taupo is the largest freshwater lake in New Zealand. On the
days before the race, during the practice swims, it had been spectacular
to swim in. On race morning, it was anything but calm. There was
so much turbulence, it looked like an ocean, not a lake. It was a cold
day and there was steady rain throughout. Visibility on the swim was
greatly reduced. When I exited the water in 1 hour and 20 minutes, I
was a little annoyed. I had thought I would go faster, and had to remind
myself to never compare times across races.

As I got on my bike, I realized that I was missing my rain jacket. I
put on as many layers as I could find, and set off. The wind picked up
and the slick streets made for a challenging ride. I was paranoid that
I was going to crash. A couple of people did crash because vision was
compromised and we had to battle a steady rain. I finished the bike
ride in over seven hours, a lot slower than my fitness indicated. I was
mentally hitting a low spot because I had worked hard on the swim and

ridden a lot in training. 'Never mind that,' I told myself, 'keep moving forward.' I picked up my trusty, familiar blue pouch. I still could not afford all the fancy gear that went with this sport and I did not care enough to shop. I started the run, feeling like complete and utter shit. Two kilometres in, my stomach started to have some issues. Within 10 km, I was in a worse place than when I had started, both mentally and physically. I told myself that quitting was not an option. I had only 32 km to run. It hit me then that I had not eaten anything since I got off my bike. The rain was cooling us down quite a bit, so I had stopped drinking as well. I tried opening the blue pouch on my waist, but the zip was stuck. I started to grab whatever I could find at the aid stations. I thought if I talked to the pouch, it might open up. So I got going on my wish list for the coming years, in some detail, albeit telepathically. I said I definitely wanted to get married, all my aunts were wrong and no, I was *still* not a lesbian. 'Oh, I also want kids … ' I said. 'I think a family is a great option, even if part-German. Do you think my mother-in-law will allow me to do all my pujas in peace?' Thankfully, the pouch did not talk back. Some questions are better left unanswered.

My hair was a wet mess and I couldn't see much, even on the run. The rain had decided it would have its way and just kept coming down. At the 20-km mark, my pouch miraculously opened up and I discovered the reason the zip had been stuck. My missing rain jacket had been unceremoniously stuffed in there. I used the jacket to warm up and wore a hairband I found in there, to keep my hair out of my face. I smiled to myself, thinking of the hairband. I have an aversion to mirrors, make-up and moisturizers. My hair maintenance issues are legendary. I recalled one instance when I was walking down a busy street in Madras with my mother, when a street vendor jumped out of one of the stalls and said, *'Seepu veenuma, papa?'* (Do you want to buy a comb, baby?). I thought it was strange that of the million people passing by, he had picked me. My mother thought it was a sign that even a shopkeeper could spot the crow's nest atop my head.

My mood was infinitely better by the 30-km mark. In the last 10 km, I picked up the pace. I was eager to get done and comb my hair. I crossed the finish line in 12 hours and 47 minutes, including transition time, with a four-hour run. I had beaten my personal best of thirteen hours by thirteen minutes. I was really happy to be done. I hung around the finish line for a while, eating whatever I could find. Then I collected my bags and ambled towards my hotel. After a quick shower, I ordered the biggest pizza they had for dinner.

I could not sleep that night. Something had gone amiss on that race. I knew I was much fitter than the timing indicated. I couldn't understand what was missing. The next day, I learned that I had come in thirtieth on the run. The run is the hardest leg of an Ironman. I told myself to remain positive in that knowledge. I knew I had a lot more work to do on the bike and I was willing to fix that. I attended the awards ceremony in a sari and was very proud to see an Indian flag among so many others in the hall.

I spent a few days after the Ironman with Sarah Ulmer and her partner Brendan, who helped me with my bike position. I had suffered a stiff lower back for much of the race, and the training shortly afterwards was no different. After 7,500 km of riding in Christchurch and the suburbs in training for Ironman New Zealand, I knew I needed help to avoid injuring my back.

Seeking some much deserved rest, I impulsively rented a car and drove to the Waitakere ranges to spend a few days not thinking about anything. I enjoyed a spectacular few days in and around Piha Beach, famous as a surfing joint but close to several hilly trails. I walked and ran to my heart's content, winding down with evening floats in the sea and a good book. I had read that Arthur Lydiard, the iconic running coach, used to train his group here and I could see why. The grounds were spectacular. Lydiard had popularized distance running and prescribed fearless mileage to his protégés, who included the legendary Kiwi runners Peter Snell and Rod Dixon. One of my favourite books in sort, and there aren't that many, is a novel titled *Once a Runner*, outlines the dedication it takes to be any good. I had always Lydiard training the protagonist in that book, successfully

After accepting the peripeteia offered by the bounty of rest in the Waitakere ranges, I returned to Christchurch, richer in perspective and proud of my latest finish. I wrote a report in my journal to keep the memory of my second most positive race and promised myself that I would persevere with my commitment to the sport.

At the university in Christchurch, I had run into Keegan on one of my first few runs around the campus. Knowing nothing of him or his marathon record, I said, 'I am really unfit, but I hope that will change soon.' He responded with, 'Ah! I am really fit and I hope that will not change soon.' I had to listen carefully at first to understand his Kiwi accent, but Keegan turned out to be pure gold in my life in the years to come. We ran together on the first day we met, and I discovered that he was exceptionally down-to-earth, with a quirky sense of humour. He had just finished a PhD from Cambridge and was working in Christchurch. The university was his alma mater too, and he and his father were part of the running group that set off on weekly runs from campus. I would later find out that the marathon he won in Christchurch was run in a time of 2 hours and 21 minutes. I could never keep up with him on any of our training runs, but we formed a great friendship. In the years that followed, I often found myself seeking him out when I hit a snag with my PhD, my training, or both. While he was a pure runner, his attitude and good humour were important in keeping my mind connected to the difficult goals I was pursuing. His father, Matthew, was another blessing in my life. The Hoopers were extremely hospitable and a fun family to be around. I was happy to be included in their little group, very aware of the fact that I was not as fast, but that my effort was well appreciated. That is why runners in general are my favourite kind of athletes – big hearts, no fuss.

Chinese Checkers

Ni Hao!
—Chinese for 'hello'.

I started working on a few more ideas for research papers and experiments in the lab, but I felt my bike performance in New Zealand could have been a lot better. Five-and-a-half weeks after a satisfying race at Ironman New Zealand, I found myself on a flight to Haikou, China. The idea of doing two Ironman races six weeks apart seemed like a fun adventure in testing my abilities, both physical and mental. So I found very affordable tickets and decided that a new laptop could wait.

China was nothing like India, but the people in the rural parts appeared to share similar circumstances. Haikou had plenty of green rice fields and wonderful people. I got to hitch a ride on a moped with a lady farmer. She was transporting some sacks of rice to a vendor. As she ferried me and her sacks past a local protest by farm labourers, I thought I was in heaven. Strangely, at the race check-in, I could see no Chinese women. The Asian women I ran into were mostly Americans or ex-pats from Hong Kong and the Far East. I wondered what that meant.

Race morning dawned before I knew it and I was not stressed. I was stressed about not being stressed, but that was not too stressful. I checked my bike bottles in and literally ran to the ocean. The swim was a two-loop event and even though I thought of several reasons to stop swimming, I never did. I just kept swimming and before I knew it, the swim was over in about an hour and twenty-seven minutes, seven minutes slower than my time at Ironman New Zealand. *Great.* I thought to myself, *I knew I should have been more stressed! This is not a picnic, Vaidyanathan. Look alive.* Once on my bike, I felt great after getting past the first 15 km or so, and felt in perfect harmony with the pace. No pain, no complaints, and no loss of focus. The bike course wound through some villages and I would not have swapped this part of the course for all the money in the world. The crowd was very supportive, the kids cheering us on were beautiful, and every time we smiled, they would cheer enthusiastically. I was flying according to the speedometer. The temperature kept rising steadily, and the second lap was a little more challenging than the first because I had to stop to get Gatorade and water at every aid station. The volunteers were similar to the volunteers in Bangalore during my first-ever half-marathon. They had no idea what they were doing. I did not realize it when I was riding, but the temperature had climbed to 30 degrees Celsius by the midway point. I wasn't happy stopping to get my fluids because it was eating up precious time, but I had no choice in the matter. I finished the ride in 6 hours and 40 minutes, twenty minutes faster than at Ironman New Zealand, and got off my bike feeling dizzy, but happy. The heat had settled at 35 degrees Celsius and 80-90 per cent humidity, and pretty soon I was radiating heat. The asphalt road seemed to be steaming, and a wall of heat cloaked me on the run. One of the competitors took a fifteen-minute swim on the beach during the run, to cool off.

I ran the whole course believing I was in the third place in my age group. Turned out I was fourth, but I had run twenty-seven minutes faster than the woman who placed third. I had no issues with that. I had worked on my bike and swim consistently for about six months and I had to keep that in perspective – the run would always be my strongest event. I ran the last 5 km in twenty-seven minutes and I knew that if I had not barfed twice during the run, I could have done it much faster. I tried multiplying seventeen and seventeen in my mind, but I did not succeed. I played Scrabble instead and rearranged big words into smaller words. The word 'EARTH' was my favourite because it had 'HEAR', 'HEAT', 'HEART', 'RATE' and 'EAT' in it.

I stayed in China for two days after the race, ending my trip with a 2,300-step speed walk around the Great Wall. I knew then that *The Art of War* was not to be taken lightly. Back on the flight to Christchurch, I was fired up to keep competing because I knew I had performed really well under difficult weather conditions, and soon after completing Ironman New Zealand. I reset my expectations on time and took in the fact that I was enjoying myself immensely. I was balancing difficult goals, felt excited and inspired, and that made it all worth it.

I would return to China the following year, looking forward to a decent race in Haikou. There were still no women from China, even in the second edition. And luck had other people to favour with a new swim course, on Nandu River, making plans of its own. I ended up hitting my head on a crew boat owing to a strong current, and racing with a concussion for over twelve hours before getting too dizzy to continue and being pulled out by a doctor. I thought that was rather funny, and what was even funnier were the visitors from English-speaking countries complaining about travel and racing conditions in the Third World. I thought about the Chinese farmer I had hitched a ride with the previous year. Both she and I listened to the beat of only one drummer, in our own heads. She didn't have to speak English for me to realize how much more empowered she was than these silly travellers with their bike bags, complaining about botulism.

DEATH AND LIFE

Steepness in Seattle

Daphne: 'I'm sorry, Frasier. I guess after a little champagne we got into the mood, and into the nude, and into the tub. But don't worry, we'll replace the candle.'
Frasier: 'If only you could replace the image.'

—*Shutout in Seattle*, Frasier

Working at the Human Interface Technology Lab (HIT Lab) in Christchurch was the highlight of my graduate education. Besides their founder Tom Furness, an absolute visionary, the lab's two bases, one in Seattle and another in Christchurch, had an eclectic collection of talent working towards creating usable, commercialized technology.

During my first winter in New Zealand, in May 2008, I accepted an invitation to visit Seattle, thinking that it would be warmer there than where I was. It was unfortunate that the invitation only arrived after I had turned down my slot at the World Championships in Florida, but I didn't worry too much about that. Instead, I planned a brief stopover at a three-day trade show in Virginia en route to Seattle, where we held a demo of one of PatNMarks' products.

The conference venue was very close to Shenandoah National Park, which came as a revelation and made the high airline fee I had to pay for my bike box totally worth it. The park is a part of the Blue Ridge Mountains, which is a part of the Appalachians. I thought it was very special to be back in the area because it was approximately four years since I had driven past the same mountains, feeling defeated. I recalled my road trip from Raleigh to Madison during the Christmas break, driving through the storm in my car Sal, with Soul Asylum playing on the radio. All of those memories came rushing back to me when I went riding in the evenings. Climbing more than a thousand metres on each ride, I spent that weekend with my bike. So many things had changed in four years. I had my self-respect back. I had a paid research position, and I no longer borrowed money to pay rent. I had carved out a brand new identity. I was an endurance athlete and an entrepreneur. I did not feel anything except a sense of relief at having made the right choices. To leave behind a life in the company of those I cherished had not been easy, but it had been the right thing to do. Without my independence, financially, mentally and otherwise, I would have been even more lost.

I woke up early, rode a few hours, and hit the trade show by 10 a.m. On the second day, I gave a talk on one of the databases we had created at PatNMarks. It was well received and the audience was clearly curious about where we were headed. I thanked my stars I hadn't accepted any external funding for the company. With a small start-up, too many cooks not only spoil the broth, they also change its very composition. At the end of those three days, Friday to Sunday, that I spent exploring Virginia, I felt completely satisfied with the ground I had covered, the people I had met and the 350 km of scenery I had the privilege of exploring from the seat of my bike.

Getting on a plane to Seattle, I was in high spirits. I had my second glimpse of the Pacific Northwest and the famed Olympic mountains as we flew across the continent. When I had visited Alaska with Aurora almost half a decade earlier, in late 2002, we had made a pit stop in Seattle before heading towards Anchorage. A trip to Alaska as a graduation gift was the easiest decision we had made. My best friend and I loved the outdoors. She loved to walk and I loved to run. We enjoyed each other's company and just goofing around. We went on a day trip that took us close to the base of the Sleeping Lady, Mount Sustina, who, according to legend, had vowed to sleep till her beloved returned from war. We both thought that was funny, since our own sleep was always rationed. I slept well, but I was a poor sleeper. Aurora was the same, but she was a deep sleeper, so much so that one night, when I stuck post-its between her toes, she did not so much as stir.

We camped for ten days at the Eagle River campground. We ran into Chris Brown, the US Olympic hopeful, at a local race held by the Skinny Ravens Run Club. Running alongside her was motivation enough to never give up.

Aurora and I had shrieked and looked at each other with glee on our first sighting of Alaska, as the plane coasted around the Chugach Mountains, cloaked in snow. Armed with a backpack, our favourite books and sturdy shoes, we had taken the bus to our campground in Anchorage. We lived in a tent, walked for hours during the day, and read in the evenings after a meagre ration of Ramen noodles, which cost close to 60 cents per packet in Alaska. If everything was bigger in Texas, everything was super expensive in Alaska.

One of the books I had picked up for my trip was *Into the Wild*, in which author Jon Krakauer narrates the story of Chris McCandless. I had picked up the book because it was on sale and sounded interesting. But Chris McCandless's espousal of a life in the wilderness, his loneliness, seemed daunting to me. As Aurora and I stomped around, we discussed the book and I did not appreciate the physicality of the pursuit. It sounded far-fetched to us at the time. Furthermore, we both sought out strong friendships. One of our aunts had raised my brother and me when we were very young and our childhood had included a lot of time spent outdoors, swimming in the Kudamurutti river, near Ayymapetai. The wilderness was always welcome, but in small doses and with ample company.

By the time I got to Seattle in the summer of 2008, some of this had changed. One look at the evergreen forests set my heart soaring. Forests were my happy place and they still are. Landing in Seattle, I had the same thought that I had when I landed in Alaska – *Expect them inclines!* I had forgotten about Chris McCandless, but I quickly found out that Krakauer was a legend in climbing and lived in Seattle. Seattle seemed to be an adventure-magnet. I also had the great pleasure of running into Chris Ragsdale, an epic randonneur (a randonée being an unsupported bike ride), and learning about Aaron Scheidies, a blind triathlete. Both men called Seattle their home.

Being back in the US was, at least initially, a little unsettling. I had wondered if it would be tough on me, whether I would be able to get in touch with my old friends, whether they would have outgrown me, and me them. But I found I had no reason to worry because most of them were happy to hear from me, genuinely proud of my progress, and eager to swap life stories and milestones.

Within days of landing in Seattle, I found an apartment with a few other students at the lab. Very soon, I was living with kind and generous roommates and a green parrot called Chewy. Once, the parrot went missing for a whole hour, having managed to fly out the open front door, and my roommate and I wandered around like crazy people, whistling and repeatedly calling out 'Chewy!' into nothingness. My roommate looked even nuttier than he was in real life, with his binoculars hanging around his neck, and we ended up with some rather appalled neighbours.

Meanwhile, my best friend in Madison, Dan, had returned from Swaziland after a stint with the Peace Corps. He had seen and learned a lot from that way of life and had a lot of great adventures to narrate. Unfortunately, the reason he was back was because he had been diagnosed with glioblastoma, a rare, malignant brain tumour, and had to be airlifted to the United States for intensive care.

It took me a while to come to terms with what was happening to Dan. Here was this tall, handsome boy, born to be a basketball player and a heart-breaker, with a unique perspective on the world. He was artistic and all-embracing in the way he lived, and even now, he never behaved like life had denied him anything. He had known me since the time I was chubby, sporting 60s' clothing and bandanas on rides. We had shared several bike rides together in Madison, on one of which he had held out an arm, his palm supporting my back, to propel me up a hill on a particularly gruelling 160-km ride.

I got in touch with Dan's mom, Lisa, and heard about a birthday party for him. I couldn't help smiling. Dan may be fighting for his life, but he was also planning a party on 7 June: he had been airlifted out of Swaziland exactly a year earlier, on that date. His short-term memory had begun to fail him by now and the chemo was wearing him out. He'd had several other problems to confront in quick succession, including a weakening eyesight, and he was on drugs that were in the clinical trial phase in the US. This was as far as a disease could test someone's will. But my friend wasn't one for giving up. He was, instead, riding when he could, with his mother crewing for him, and training for a local sprint triathlon. I knew I would not miss being at his birthday party for anything in the world. I had to find a way to make it back to Madison.

I made my plans and bought tickets on a red-eye flight with the intention of surprising him. On 6 June, Dan's mother emailed me to say that he had passed away the day before. I wrote back through tears, telling her I would like to be at the funeral. But I never got on that plane. A combination of grey skies and desperation cloaked me in grief such that I did not know I was capable of experiencing.

I hated myself all of a sudden. I should have written to Dan more often. I should have gotten out to Madison a week in advance. Until that point, I thought I had re-invented myself, but grappling with Dan's demise, I realized that I had become a different person. I no longer had illusions about an academic career or any cutting-edge research I was going to be a part of. I had no long-term relationships to speak of. I had tried and failed to cultivate any lasting friendships after my time in Madison.

It was true that as I grew older, it got harder and harder to trust people. Dan, on the other hand, had still seemed capable of dreaming. All the time he was in Swaziland, a part of me was thrilled to know him. The year he had been diagnosed, I had been a lousy friend because I was a wimp. I feared personal loss so much that I decided I would not deal with it. Here was a guy who rode hundreds of miles to help people in need. He raised money for causes he cared about. Yet, thanks to the tumour, he had started worrying about finishing a 20-km bike ride for fear of not being able to see properly. Life seemed unbearably cruel. But I finally admitted one thing to myself – I was wrong to think that I was better off alone. I was just more comfortable living in my self-involved chasm of self-improvement. But I had stopped enjoying solitude sans friendships a long time ago. I realized that I had a huge responsibility to not forget what Dan meant to me. What his way of living did for the people around him. What his attitude brought to my life directly. What his relationship with his mother showed me about love. Lisa had raised him almost single-handedly and he had never let her down.

In the weeks that followed, I felt strangely detached from everything. I felt like I could not handle the emptiness. As though mirroring my mood, it rained constantly in Seattle. I started running to work every morning on the Burke-Gilman trail, right outside where I was renting a room. Biking was out of the question and on some days I felt like I could not look at my bike the same way anymore. It reminded me of Dan, the rides we had been on, the laughter we had shared, the stories we had swapped. I seriously considered going to a psychologist after Dan's death. There were some very, very bleak days. When I got into my lab one day, soaked after what had been the second week of non-stop rain and burst into tears, I decided I needed help. If I was too proud to seek out an actual therapist, I would at the very least educate myself.

Seattle was littered with bookstores. I picked up a thin volume called *Man's Search for Meaning* by Viktor Frankl, on one of my stops at a second-hand store. I had read a lot about logotherapy and wanted to understand more. Frankl was one of the earliest proponents of this method of healing, which emphasized *meaning* as being central to any human being's journey through life. Frankl was a revelation to me. I read the whole book the same night I bought it. The story of him surviving the Holocaust and not losing hope in the heart of despair was enough to make me continue reading. The basic premise of the book was that a person can only choose how they react to their circumstantial truth or suffering, they cannot control or avoid suffering, although suffering can, and does, bring out unbelievable grace and humility in people. Frankl keeps reminding the reader that he is a highly qualified intellectual, like several others who were sent to the concentration camps. He could, and should have, failed to rationalize where this left him, but by choosing to imagine an alternate reality and his own longevity in a positive manner, he survived the bleak conditions in four different camps, including Auschwitz. I put that book down in the early hours of the morning, laced up my shoes, and ran straight to the university library. I picked up all the books I could find by Viktor Frankl, took the bus home, and read all of them the same week. I did not leave my room except to eat and drink water. Among other things, Frankl explains the empiricism that athletes experience with goal-setting. This frees them up from dependence on commerce or the meaningless pursuit of goals, which depend on other people's validation. This made a lot of sense to me. At the end of the week, I realized I had not cried the whole time I had been reading. Nor did I set out for a run once I was done. I packed the books neatly into my backpack to return to the library and went to watch a movie, something I had not done in almost five years.

I woke up the next day, drowning in a sea of regret and self-loathing. The voice of Edna, from *The Incredibles*, was playing in my head: 'My God, you've gotten fat. Come in, come, come!' It was noon by the time I rolled into the gym and got on the treadmill. Through my run, I recalled the voice of Elastigirl shouting, 'India-Golf Niner-Niner, transmitting in the blind guard – disengage, repeat, disengage!' I focused on disengaging from the pain inside me. When I got off the treadmill, I was rosy-cheeked, burning bright, and ready for my cool-down swim. I looked like a total wreck, but I loved every minute of the painful hobble towards the pool. I felt great after the swim and decided that this was not the end of my day. I had to ride my bike. I told myself that Dan would have wanted me to. After buying nearly a whole rack of energy bars, I hooked up with a group that evening and we started on a hilly 50-km loop. There were six hills in the loop, with an average climbing time of ten minutes per hill, the incline progressively going up from 6 per cent to 17 per cent. With names like Death Trap, Guillotine and Goat Hill, they sure lived up to their billing. Goat Hill was the ultimate humdinger. It had five sharp hairpin bends followed by what felt like vertical walls, and getting through them was exhausting. I felt delusional and almost quit at the twenty-five-minute mark, when we had our first flat. A girl I met on the ride kept repeating, 'Come on, what's a little pain?' I was certain that she was the devil incarnate. The Goat was optional, but the view from the top, including a very distant Mount Rainier, which I had renamed Rainy-er, the shimmering sunset, and the company of six people who knew what it meant to push themselves beyond their limits, made it all worthwhile. The ride ended around 9.30 p.m. and by then, all thoughts of exhaustion were gone. The group gathered for Mexican food and I discovered that I indeed had a hollow-leg when it came to enchiladas. Being in the company of people my age helped me. These people had the same questions about life and exactly the same difficulty with real-estate prices ruling the world. I told myself that the day I began to get serious about real-estate prices, I would retire from sport.

In my first few years in sport, I used to think that the highest form of suffering was having to sit in a sports psychologist's office for a mandatory session to get to my Olympic Gold a little later in life. Of all the bells and whistles that came with modern-day sport, until that point I had found shrinks who psychoanalysed sporting egos to be the most entertaining. I had a problem with my temper for a few weeks before Ironman New Zealand. It would go off without warning when I was out by myself in the boonies with my aerobars and a painful lower back. I would mostly get really negative and furious for all of fifteen minutes, drink some water, and keep riding. When the problem persisted for four weeks and my support crew began to crack, I walked into a sports psychologist's office and was given a lecture about visualization, circle of control, what you can affect and cannot affect, choosing your actions, etc. At the end of that hour, I thought this would be a nice profession for me to think about twenty years down the line. It paid a neat amount and I could do monologues. But I realized what purgatory really meant that evening, after we had ridden up Goat Hill. It was me, getting over my rigid thought processes and accepting that there was a place for a little existentialism, logotherapy and, most importantly, Viktor Frankl, in *everyone's* life. The mind needed to heal; life's pressures were hard enough to deal with. Changing your mind sometimes was not a bad idea.

That summer in Seattle, instead of sitting around in stuffy rooms or getting angry with my back or whatever was bothering me, I decided to make some friends and read a few books to get me past my existential woes. Of all the writers I read, and re-read, the two Jacks – London and Kerouac – John Steinbeck and Billy Collins were my favourites. But it was Viktor Frankl who had a simple explanation for why my generation was so restless and unwilling to settle: the grand challenges of survival were absent because we were children of luxury. I thought back to my own discontentment in Bangalore, in leading a life without any challenges. The take-home message from this brilliant author was that freedom degenerates into arbitrariness unless it is counter-balanced with responsibility. I had to wonder what I was in the sport for. If it was not a hobby or a lifestyle that I was pursuing, what was it? While, on the outside, it seemed chaotic to try and chase milestones I could not explain, this level of entropy was, in fact, a good thing. I was happiest when I was working hard towards difficult goals. I was also happy to attribute my pursuits in sport to a little day-to-day unhappiness about inequalities, a short temper, or dissatisfaction about being handed a certain draw.

In fashioning a mission statement, I decided to listen to the Dalai Lama, who said that 'Sleep is the best meditation'. By that standard, I had probably already attained nirvana. I had been sleeping like a pregnant hippo in Seattle. Pregnant with twins whom I intended to name 'mysteriously' and 'quiet'. In my sleep, I had feature-film-length dreams about how little I had accomplished with my time in the last year. These dreams were complete with voice-overs from the overbearing swim coach from Bangalore, his beer belly wobbling with laughter as he mocked me and my goals: 'Who leaves home to be a better athlete? Get real! Indians don't have hobbies. You are STILL not married? *Che che che.*' My dreams often ended with random thoughts like the propensity for laughter of tall trees in the Pacific Northwest, various birdsongs sung by Chewy and friends, or finding myself in a world-famous triathlete's garage with some industrial size blenders and shelves filled with exotic fruits. The prime-time dream featured Denzel Washington reading me a bedtime story.

I slowly came to terms with the fact that I had just experienced a deep and personal loss with Dan's sudden demise. I was sad for a while and then, re-reading Dan's letters to me, I had a slow return out of grief. Ursula Le Guin's words came back to me: 'To learn which questions are unanswerable, and not to answer them: this skill is most needful in times of stress and darkness.' Honestly, it's easy to be miserable, and difficult to be optimistic and happy. So I decided to go with the latter. I would overcome the difficulty and not allow self-doubt, my constant companion, to get the better of me. I was determined to get out of the funk I found myself in.

Since I was not one for material gifts, I decided that the best way to celebrate Dan's life was to organize a training camp. Work on my PhD was picking up and slogging like a zombie made it easier to handle the demanding hours. On a particularly memorable Thursday, which included a 3.5-km swim, a two-hour run, an hour of commuting on the bike, and thirty minutes of upper-body weights, the camp officially kicked off. The plan was to swim 10 km on Friday, in three swim sessions spaced through the day, ride 320 km on Saturday from Seattle to Portland, and finish up on Sunday with a three-hour run. Any extra sessions would be icing on the cake. Of course, given that I was in Seattle, which was twelve hours behind India, I also had to take client calls at unexpected times. Thursday night was no different, and at 2 a.m., I had a conversation that went as follows:

Client: 'Anu, did you get the samples I sent you? I personally like the lilac-scented one.'

Me: 'Yes, sir, I got it, all fifteen aromas for the anti-balding and anti-wrinkle creams. That's quite impressive.'

Client: 'Now, the trademark application, has this been processed?'

Me: 'Yes, Mr S, the trademark for your anti-balding cream has been processed.'

Client: 'Good! Good! Very good! So, how are you? All fine with your research?'

Me: 'I am very well, thanks.'

Client: 'So, which sample did you like best? Lilac or Morning Flower?'

Me: 'Sir, sorry to disappoint you, but I have not tried the free samples
you sent me…'

Client: 'Was the scent too strong? See, I could not decide…'

Me: 'Oh … no, no, it smells fine. I am just not balding yet, so I might
have to wait.'

Client: 'Yes, yes, but you can try it on the front of the forehead if you
wish. '

Me: 'Mmm.'

Client: 'What time is it for you? '

Me: 'Oh, it's about 2.30 a.m.'

Client: 'Ayyo! Sorry, Anu. Go to sleep.'

Me: 'No problem, I don't sleep anyway. Good night!'

Understandably, after this, waking up at 5 a.m. for a swim on Friday
was a mammoth task. The public pool was peaceful, though, and once
my head stopped spinning from the lack of sleep, I was actually quite
happy to be swimming. The first session was over before I knew it,
and I was back that afternoon for the senior swim session, where the
minimum age of swimmers was at least fifty-five. The chlorine was
starting to get to me and the 3×1,000 metre set I had to swim descending,
which meant each successive 1,000 had to be faster than the previous
one, was not my idea of fun. However, these senior swim sessions are a
hoot, especially because they help put things in perspective. There was
a loud argument on the other side of the pool about how floral shorts
were so last season. After session 1 and 2, I had a panic attack and ate
some bread to get over it. Session 3 was another boxing match with
some very rude men in the pool, who had a problem with me watching
the clock. But I got through it. The switch to swimming three times
a day was a real learning curve in terms of attire. I realized that two
swimsuits would absolutely not suffice for my swim wardrobe and yes,
floral designs were so last season.

I was so relieved after the three swims that I went on a ninety-minute run to forget about the time spent underwater, and so ended up executing a fourth, unplanned training session for that day. *Pride and Prejudice* was on TV that night and I had to watch it because I find Darcy's sideburns delectable, and Kiera Knightley is an absolute fright with her hairstyle. Midnight rolled in again before I knew it and I was still wide awake, too wired to sleep. Damn those floral prints.

The next day I went on a 320-km ride from Seattle to Portland. It wasn't long before I started to regret the drive to the start line because I was so sleepy. I was very sure that I was going to turn back at the 50-km mark and sensibly get some sleep. Also, I was running on empty and that makes for bad moods. But at the first-aid station, I heard someone say, 'I'm turning back because I'm not betting on the weather.' I think that lit a fire in me and I turned up the pace, to complete 160 km with negative splits. Even in my unfashionable attire, which included a thick sweatshirt and a woollen cap, I was perfectly all right with the weather. We had an overnight stop in Centralia, Washington. As I sat in a sleeping bag in the roomy gymnasium, it felt good to disconnect from the world, even if it was just for one night. I knew a few people from the group rides in Seattle and we spent the evening chatting and swapping life stories. The fascination with my nose-ring and deep tan acted as a conversation starter.

I discovered that Seattle had an eclectic population, including some really phenomenal athletes balancing day jobs and sport. Unlike Kiwis, Americans, in my opinion, lived at a breakneck pace and had a lot more to deal with in their daily lives. For such a rich nation, America has a woefully broken healthcare system and almost no reliable public transport to speak of. Listening to the experiences of the commuters themselves was interesting. I felt a lot better hearing that their struggles were similar to mine, chasing after excellence past the hamster wheel of market economics and broken systems. I started to understand what motivated some of them to ride. I also learned about measuring inclines and was impressed by my riding mates' encyclopaedic knowledge of terrain. I decided to learn a little more on my own rides. On this particular ride, we were climbing nearly 5,000 feet over a number of rollers. We finished the session in sunny Portland the next day and got on a bus to Seattle soon after.

A three-hour run the same evening was just too much for me to handle. The sun was out bright and shining, everything was fine and dandy. I even had on my $8 Louis Garneau sleeveless top, bought on sale at the local tri-store and touted as a miracle garment. But nothing helped. I had to pull the plug at 2 hours and 35 minutes and hobble back home. I went to bed early, at 10.30 p.m.

After this self-imposed camp, I started riding again. I met some lovely people in Seattle and rode all over town. My new best friends, Burke and Gilman (the Burke-Gilman trail), greeted me every morning till the day I left Seattle.

Later that summer, I participated in the Lake Stevens Half Ironman, which was held on a challenging course in Everett, Washington, 40 km north of Seattle. My training leading up to the race was satisfactory, but I ate at a local diner for the first time in two weeks and ended up with a high fever four days before the race. I had a choice to make. I could withdraw participation and come back empty-handed, or I could do the race to the best of my abilities and not be bothered by the result. The only problem with a fever is that one has to wait till the very end to see if it goes down and stays down, and swimming is not a great activity to indulge in during this time. I slept most of Wednesday through Saturday and went on a little run on Saturday evening. I felt fine on that run and decided that I may not have my best race, but I loved this sport too much to not participate if I could. I ended up with the same result I had in Geelong, except for a few minutes lost on the hilly bike course and a few minutes on the run due to sheer exhaustion. I felt great, however, and ended at thirteenth place on the run, placing twenty-sixth overall. I had finished in six hours on a much hillier course compared to Geelong and that was good enough to write home about.

Moonstone Trails

To strive, to seek, to find, and not to yield
— 'Ulysses', Tennyson

I left Seattle grudgingly. I was just beginning to make new friends there, learning the cycling and running routes by heart, and also learning to swim alongside the fifty-five-and-over veterans at the community pools. It felt like I was in a big jigsaw puzzle with pieces from New Zealand and Seattle standing out in stark contrast, strung together by a crackerjack dream of consistent training and racing.

In Seattle, I had run into a diverse set of scientists in my lab and associated research groups. I was armed with a rock-solid plan for my doctoral work. And I had a brand-new perspective on the word 'incline'.

I returned to New Zealand in early September 2008 and rented the first place I could find in Christchurch. It was a house on top of a hill, in the middle of my favourite bike route in the world, up Gebbies Pass, which was a steep offshoot from Dyers Pass.

My roommates in the new house, three men and two women, were anything but athletic and that was precisely why I moved in there. I wanted balance in my life. I was ready to crash and burn while keeping it real. The house had paper-thin walls and the rent was dirt-cheap. One morning, I woke up wondering what 'it' was about. Was 'it' about infamy? Perhaps 'it' was about immortality? Surely, 'it' was a tidal wave or a moonstone-coloured asteroid that would take me to a place where I could finally say, 'I'm home! I belong!'

That day, on my run, I thought about the small housewarming party

I'd organized to which I had invited all my Kiwi friends, including Drew of the hot-pink-speedo fame. Drew had run into a tree while riding his mountain bike, earning him the title of tree-hugger, and I was chuckling to myself as I ran, thinking about this. My route was flat for the first 500 metres along the promenade, after which there was a sharp climb for about 800 metres, to a road that descended into Taylor's Mistake, a little cove. After that, the tar road ended and it was mostly dirt tracks that went uphill for around 5 km, leading onto Summit Road, with its sharper inclines, which led into Evans Pass, which descended back into Sumner. The entire run was around 17 to 20 km, depending on where one started.

I completed the first incline in record time and was thrilled. My previous best time on this route had been eight months ago, when I thought I was pretty fit. Today, I decided to really go for it, without being afraid of twisting an ankle in the undergrowth or worrying about other consequences. I started to remember things about my dear old father, who was probably one of the hippie generation. He pampered me rotten and always told me I could do whatever I wanted to. In his own inimitable style, he often sang, 'It's better to burn out than to fade away.' So I guess crashing and burning was part of my DNA.

By this time, I was chuckling and playing the piano with my feet, with the rocks on the moonstone-coloured trails that led to the topmost section of my run. The views on Godley Head Track were spectacular, even on the wettest day. With a total elevation of around 1,500 feet, parts of the run were risky. Sheer cliffs rose up 120 metres from the sea and many parts of the track had no railings. I was alert and rested that day, so I managed fine. I got to the halfway point fifteen minutes faster than I had been averaging all month, when running on no sleep. Next up were two long U-turns on the road, which I called 'the twin-twisters'. The twins were long turns on Summit Road, and flat. Past the twins came the portion of the road I called the trickster. The trickster couldn't be estimated too well because it curved too many times and the mind was too tired to grasp things at this point. When I got to the summit, the sky had turned from orange to mauve to purple. There were five trees that lined the horizon after I ran the trickster. They kept me company, talked to me when the weather was bad and encouraged me at all times. These five trees stood in one line on the opposite cliff, and to me they resembled my family, my best friend and a former coach, all important people in my life, without whom the world would be so much more difficult to navigate. I fashioned those five trees and me to be the Sultans of Spring. I felt like I was dancing, not running. I usually don't run hard downhill, but on that day I did. My heart was in my mouth. I must have looked ridiculous to the two startled mountain bikers I passed, gasping for air, my face totally wracked with pain. It took all my focus to keep running hard, but I shaved a whole five minutes on the entire distance from my previous best time, in April. It had taken eight months to get five minutes faster. If that did not teach me patience, nothing could.

When I finished, I swore and doubled over on the beach. I had to get some water and orange juice from the local supermarket, immediately. An old lady, who was ahead of me, wanted me to leave the long line at the checkout and get her a different bottle of juice or milk than the one she had. I said sorry and refused to cooperate. All I wanted was to get out of there in a hurry, I was ready to pass out. This sport had no points for being a team player. I walked back down to the beach and stood there for fifteen minutes, watching the waves clap by, and realized that 'it' was about personal satisfaction. When I was running, nobody knew that I was working on beating my time and testing my limits and I didn't want anyone to know either. This was about me, and the clock.

As the months rolled by, living in the house became a little problematic. My roommates kept long hours and while they were respectful of each other's schedules, the walls, floorboards and kitchen were not as accommodating. The floors would creak incessantly as people came in and left during the day, making for a rather noisy space. While every athlete espouses strict discipline and 5 a.m. wake-up calls, I was inclined to think that a foolish consistency and an inflexible regime with the same wake-up time every single day was for the birds. So I changed my training routine around, often running home at

10 p.m. and starting a little later than normal in the mornings. Spring was particularly wet and I found myself enjoying running in the rain. Seattle had done wonders to my attitude and water-proofed my soul for life.

In the long run, however, I started to fall sick, owing to a combination of broken sleep and lackadaisical kitchen hygiene, which was not up to my Iyer-girl standards by any measure. The problem with cooking is that one also needs to wash up and have clean utensils at one's disposal. Most of my roommates were very good about taking care of things as soon as they could. One was a single parent and I definitely knew his priorities were in the right place. I didn't see any point in complaining, but I knew I had to move out.

The week I decided to move out, I had suffered a major attack of food poisoning and was in bed for four days straight. I never realized that a bit of bacteria could cause so much trouble. I had a lot of time to think between napping twenty hours a day and found myself caught in a sea of regret and self-loathing. I took the opportunity of being confined to my bed to read Mark Twain's *The Tragedy of Pudd'nhead Wilson* and smiled through it. I also re-read Emerson's essay, 'Self-Reliance', which I had first read when I was in the throes of making a very big decision in my life. One that involved moving continents, not taking any shit from snooty men, and starting my own company. It felt like I was on the brink of another major life change, so Emerson was on my bedside again.

I had changed pools. I no longer swam at the QE2 as it was too far from the hills and my new place. I was dying to impress the swim coach at my new pool on the first day I got out of bed. She resembled Dory from the movie *Finding Nemo* and her motto was, 'Just keep swimming, just keep swimming'. I swam 2 km on Monday with major nausea and Tuesday, I was back in the emergency room for blood tests. Wednesday, I swam twice for a total of 6 km. Thursday was Christmas, and I ran for just a few hours. I had a work deadline to meet on Monday, so I clocked in forty hours of work between Friday and Saturday with no sleep. Saturday evening, I swam 3.5 km till the pool closed and they threw me out. I followed this up with a ninety-minute rumble in the hills. I wanted to swim an 8.5-km session to round off my training for the week. But my roommate had been practising midnight Tae Bo and that kept me up until 2 a.m. I could only curse the lack of sound proofing in the house.

I woke up around 10.30 a.m. on Sunday and lay in bed thinking. Finally, I got out the door at noon and went for a little ride. The wind was on my back and I had a fantastic ride lasting less than three hours. Usually, this ride took me three hours and seventeen minutes on a good day and three hours and twenty-seven minutes on a day with head-winds, so I was clearly on rocket fuel. I went to Subway for a bite and felt really good the whole time. My intestines seemed to be behaving themselves after a week of illness. I stepped into the pool and had a 3-km set written out for me by my new swim coach. She took the mystery out of swimming, so I could understand my technique and recognize when I was having a good or bad day. I got through 4-km in one hour and forty-five minutes and was hungry again, so I had to get out, eat the rest of my sub and run to the coffee shop, to load up on the Kiwi marvel called jet-planes, a category of Kiwi confectionary with a lot of sugar. When I got back in the pool within thirty minutes and swam the rest of the 4.5-km in one hour and forty minutes, the last 1,000 metres being the fastest, I found a floating five-dollar bill in the pool and took that to be a sign. Five dollars for an 8.5-km swim, not a bad paycheque. I got out of the pool, my arms feeling like soufflé, but all that swimming had made my legs really antsy for a run. And so I bid goodbye to the day with an eighty-minute run.

Before 2009 rolled in, an old colleague from Austin wrote to me. Sam was a slightly older lady, a musician who had lived most of her life out of a suitcase. She had travelled all over Europe and the world, performing. Sam and I had struck up a friendship because we both loved music, thunderstorms, warm rain and a particularly delicious organic sandwich, which we often bought for lunch at a local joint in Austin. In her, I saw a future version of myself, alone but not lonely, footloose and leaving on a jet plane in thirty seconds.

Sam wrote: 'Anu, dear heart, I haven't played the guitar in many months now, I don't know why. The case reproaches me quietly from my bedroom corner. But I have recently trimmed my nails to have the absolute perfect length for playing. Moderately long on the right hand and very short on the left, so I must be getting ready to play again, it's the only reason I would have bothered to trim them so short. Playing does for me what running does for you, I think. Time drops away and endorphins fill my system. It doesn't matter whether I am practising or playing seriously, it is all the same. You feel as if you are not quite of this world for a little while. It is as if the universe shifts ten degrees or so. Does that make sense? Well, maybe that's bullshit, but it is something very different from everyday life. That's my story and I'm stickin' to it.'

I understood every word she had written. I too worked hard, whether it was in sport or towards other goals, simply because it made me happy. My idea of partying involved working towards something, and I was perfectly fine being that way. As the Kiwi coach I met on my very first trip to New Zealand liked to remind us, 'If it were easy, it wouldn't be worth doing.' For me, it was all about the pursuit. I was officially out of time and patience for all things 'impossible'. I needed both my books and my bike; I would never be able to choose one over the other.

As I grew older in the sport, I realized that my expectations had changed, my reasons for participating in this sport had changed and, most of all, I had now understood that self-realization would always be a part of the package. It was no surprise that by the time New Year rolled around, I was setting personal bests on all my training routes by a wide margin.

Being a graduate student left me with precious little spare change, but one day, I proudly took my meagre savings in a little envelope to a bike store in New Zealand. My old Trek bike, Mrs Martinez, which I had been using since my first Ironman, was made of aluminum and was supremely beat up after thousands of miles of travel to races, across five different continents. It had dents the size of tennis balls and while it was a hard decision to buy a new bike, I did it because with increased training, I needed to be comfortable. Also, I felt I had earned it after half a decade in the sport. The bike-shop owner's face was blank when I told him how much I had to spend on a new carbon bike. He took me aside to his workshop and kindly told me that I would not be able to afford even the frame of a new bike with the money I had, let alone working parts. I was heartbroken. I told him I had done my research online, but he said they were bad deals, as there was no assurance on second-hand bikes sold online. However, I was in luck because New Zealand, unlike America, was not a land of materialistic excess. This shop owner had seen me coming in for several months prior, browsing the new frames and pretending I could not find what I needed before finally leaving the shop. My German engineer had gone back to Germany, and having no boyfriend came with the advantage of copious free time on weekends. What better way to spend it than at a bookstore or a bike shop?

The shop owner suggested that I buy a second-hand carbon frame, which had been ridden for exactly four months by a member of a local professional cycling team, before their bike sponsor had changed. I took his suggestion and, with the help of Shrek, rebuilt the bike. It was weird riding it at first, but eventually, I got used to it and felt I had gotten a great deal. Later on, the same bike-shop owner sponsored my clothing for all New Zealand races and gave me a big discount almost every time I walked into his store. Looking back, I would say that a considerable part of my journey involved backbreaking work, but I was lucky to be noticed by kind strangers. The adage 'The harder I work, the luckier I get' began to make sense to me over time.

Randonneuring

Bicycle bicycle bicycle
I want to ride my bicycle bicycle bicycle
I want to ride my bicycle
I want to ride my bike
I want to ride my bicycle
I want to ride it where I like.

—Queen

I was singularly unlucky in my search for good roommates once I moved out of my home on top of the hill. In the three months between January and April 2009, I moved three times after trying out three different housemates. First it was an overbearing schoolteacher, who probably took me in because I was a PhD student and was very disappointed upon discovering my sporting habits. Second was a woman who had a picture of her SUV in her living room. While I had no issue with the fact that she was a chain-smoker, she had an issue with the spices I used in the kitchen. I got so tired of packing and moving that I decided to celebrate my itinerant Bedouin-ness with a bike ride. I thought it would be a fun experiment to ride between Christchurch and Nelson, upwards of 400 km, in three days. The long Easter weekend was the best opportunity for this little adventure. I was very lonely, but too proud to invite myself to anyone's party. If I didn't feel welcome with my own roommates, how could I feel welcome anywhere else?

I set off with a small backpack containing three pairs of contact lenses, toothpaste, three sets of clothes, an extra pair of socks, one spare tube and tyre, four cans of CO2 to fill my tyres with in case of a flat, along with a manual on how to use it, and the book that has always held my heart in rapt attention, *The Call of the Wild*. There have been a couple of Jacks in my life, but the most prolific ones had the last names 'London' and 'Kerouac', the latter becoming less interesting after my teenage years, once I realized that he had been mooching off his old relatives in real life.

Without checking the weather, supremely unconcerned about the wind howling outside since 6 a.m., I set off alone with my backpack, iPod and Mrs Martinez, the Blue Bike being retired for Easter. The plan was to ride from Christchurch to Nelson. In the event that I became road-kill and needed to be thrown into a grave, or simply needed a pick-up, I had to let a few people know where I was going. That I could die in relative obscurity without offending anyone was a great relief to me. My own insignificance seemed like a blessing. I was in a fairly good mood after the realization that I was responsible for nothing but myself, and my mind became surprisingly calm and clear. I also knew that the famous Weka Pass magpie, who terrorized even the most seasoned of cyclists, was out on annual leave with his tax auditor and would not be around to bother me. I was riding and singing along and barely noticed that it was a hot day. I had to make a brief stop to mail some garbage bags I had borrowed from my SUV-idolizing roommate while moving house the night before. She had called as I set off, to tell me she needed them back. Then, all responsibilities aside, I was on my way.

An hour into the ride, I noticed that I had already gone through both my bottles of water, and that was a bit disconcerting. On top of that, the cows were simply not talking back. 'Season of mists...' I began. But there was only a passive shaking of heads and a silent murmur amongst them, about how I was talking too much. My spirits were pretty high until 80 km, at which point I had been through four bottles of water, Coke and other drinks. My mouth felt constantly dry. The bike didn't seem to be moving very fast even though I was pedalling pretty hard. I put Tupac Shakur on my music player and decided to ignore my bike.

I stopped for a quick lunch where I met a guy called Symon, with a 'y'. He gave me a great map to what was called The Great Divide – officially, the Lewis Pass, over the Southern Alps. He said it was flat riding till a place called 'Engineers Camp', after which the pass itself was 30 km long, and then it was all downhill. I knew where I was going, which was a rarity. I did not ask about the terrain, the elevation, the duration or the weather forecast, because they were just factors to be endured. I pulled into Hanmer Springs, some 160 km from where I had started riding in Christchurch. When I called my new roommate later that night, she informed me that it had been one of the hottest days in Christchurch, over 30 degrees Celsius, with 30 per cent humidity and 30 kph headwinds turning into even fiercer gusts. No wonder my bike was going so slow. I was worried about what that might have done to my legs. I thought I would ask one of my biker buddies what the Lewis Pass was like, but she had already gone to bed.

On the second day, I was too afraid to check my messages in the morning because I had a very long way to go and I didn't want to turn back. I started out before 6 a.m., wanting to make good time towards Engineers Camp. I was severely intimidated by the Lewis Pass crossing. I reasoned that if I was to climb for 30-km, I might as well do it when the sun was not at its peak. But I didn't know what to expect. I repeated the name of the pass over and over again, which kept my spirits high in anticipation. I was a little scared because I had only two bottles of water, three cold drinks and three energy bars and I didn't know what would go through my head. Turned out, times like these are the only times when nothing goes through your head. I was consumed by living in the moment, keeping my eyes on the road ahead, and beginning to understand why we do whatever it is we do. I was in this sport to stay. A Kiwi coach I had encountered used to say, 'It takes a long time to get good.' I heard that as 'It takes "along time" to get good'. I had got my wrist slapped before for not having enough friends, but that was changing. I had a list of half a dozen people I could call in case of an emergency and I was satisfied by that thought. As for posterity, I decided I would write a book called *Monkeys on Bikes* and make money off the royalties. I mean, it's got to be worth something to wear spandex with a nose-ring.

I made it to Engineers Camp forty-five minutes earlier than I had expected to. One of my bottles had fallen off and I couldn't be bothered to pick it up a third time. The sun was up, but there was some mild cloud cover, so it was tolerably cool. I met a couple who donated a bottle to my cause and also informed me that I had already climbed a fair bit, and that Engineers Camp was not the beginning of the Lewis Pass. That really helped me mentally, as the bumps till that point had not seemed like much, probably because I thought the real climbing was yet to come. I gulped down some liquid and started to climb again. There was a bit of traffic to contend with, a little water alongside the roads and some construction and gravel causing discomfort, but it was not a particularly high or steep climb after all. In Christchurch, there is a road that goes out towards Diamond Harbor, with a massive climb of about 1,300 feet. I had expected to find a similar, if not worse, gradient or incline climbing the Lewis Pass, but that wasn't the case. This one was just rollers and as one of my friends later pointed out, it had a lot of false summits. My pack was starting to feel heavy and I quickly drank up the cans of fluid in there before pulling into Springs Junction for lunch. It was another cracker of a day with the temperature hitting 34 degrees Celsius and climbing. I had not got off my bike between Hanmer and Springs Junction, except to eat at Engineers Camp. Besides, there was no place to stop.

This was also true between Springs Junction and Murchison, my final destination for the second night. I had to carry all my nutrition and fluids with me, which made for great training. There was some wind, but I was not worried. I was making good time and feeling quite strong. The fatigue kicked in during the last 30 km, as the mercury kept rising. I was also getting angrier as I got closer to the end. The heat seemed to be making me more furious by the second. I couldn't wait to take a shower. To cheer myself up, I tried to test my photography skills while riding and the results were quite pleasing. I looked at my spiffy new bike computer and saw a total elevation gain in the 5,000 feet range and fifty-three minutes. I had to remind myself that my legs had been under a lot of strain lately and could use some rest.

The guest list at my brother's wedding was pretty international for a small wedding close to our family's village. I figured it would be the last time I would meet some of my crazy aunts who kept irritating me about getting married, and the first time in many years that I would meet my favourite cousin, who lived in Houston. The wedding was in a place called Swamimalai, which is one of several temples within a 50-km radius of Kumbakonam. It's crazy that we Indians invite so many people to our weddings. Even the old German boyfriend showed up to experience first-hand why we were so hung up on marital bliss.

On that trip, I went on an early morning run from Swamimalai, past Ayyampetai and towards Thanjavur, past gods that take so many forms – Murugan, Allah, Buddha, Shiva and their beautiful wives – over a 40-km stretch. I ran for three hours on the back roads, going past a woman who screamed, 'Who are you running from?' In the dark, starless sky, somewhere between Kumbakonam and Thanjavur, where the curves in the road are strung together like jasmine flowers in a garland, each looking exactly like the one next to it but expressing a different heartache, I decided to start training for Ultraman Canada. I sent up a little prayer to the jackfruit, neem and tamarind trees that lined the highway. 'I am a woman, y'all,' I began, 'I am a short brown woman and very, very hopeful of getting to this huge race, in a country where I started this journey. After you are done helping all those who are in need, kindly accept this prayer of my intention to start Ultraman Canada.' My overbearing aunts immediately appeared in chorus in my reverie asking, 'What about this German boy? Are you going to marry him? You should have gotten married first, not your younger brother … Is Ultraman really important? You are getting old…'

I replied, 'Maybe I want to do both, Athai, can you accept that? Besides, I want to marry a Canadian, free healthcare and all.' Then my mother's sister, Sacchu, appeared saying, 'Anu, *kalyanam pannikaradu naan pon poranda madri iruku* (Anu, your getting married is like my being born a woman). You please complete your studies, find a job, then worry about getting married.' All my aunts fell silent and the gods probably smiled because I saw the sun come up through some trees on the side of a narrow highway. I was at the 13-km mark when dawn started to break. My lucky number.

After the wedding, we came back to Bangalore and went on a road trip to Mysore. We looked around the grand palace and the gardens and did a hill workout. My German boy, who had come along, looked out of the window of the bus and commented, 'Where are all the women?' We were pulling into Bangalore, late in the evening, having left Mysore four hours ago. I said, 'Yeah, where *are* all the women?' Secretly, I felt hugely relieved about not having to train on that highway again.

Following this was a three-day trip to Kerala, to visit the backwaters. We cut through Karnataka, to Coimbatore, in Tamil Nadu, and into Ernakulam, in Kerala. We made a brief stop at Fort Cochin, passing through places once visited by Vasco da Gama, and took a ferry back to the mainland to get on a train to Varkala, where we took a dip in the Arabian Sea. It was a wonderful, warm trip home. Three states, five cities and several riverbanks later, I was rejuvenated and happy. Memories of my time with good friends and a young-at-heart family were packed away in the minimal luggage which I took back to New Zealand.

Prospectors

Nothing stirred. The Yukon slept under a coat of ice three feet thick.

—*To Build a Fire*, Jack London

In June 2009, PatNMarks started a new branch in North America. Based on referrals from two clients, our footprint in the US suddenly exploded. After finishing all the paperwork, I landed in Florida to stay with a friend of a friend and train for a few weeks. I had permission from my advisor to work from elsewhere for a few weeks, I was just not sure how many weeks.

I did not take to Florida. It was flat and the place was a concrete jungle. My roommate was constantly mad at me for waking up late at 7 a.m. She was a swimmer who had almost made it to the Olympics and considered 5 a.m. wake-up calls the only true way to athletic greatness. Soon enough, the itch to hit the mountains took over and I found myself on a plane to Salt Lake City, Utah, after talking to a couple of buddies. On the plane, I was pleasantly surprised to be sitting next to a boy from Raleigh, North Carolina, where I had attended graduate school several years back. Since the flight from Orlando to Salt Lake City was rather long, we ended up talking about everything. Bad music, long hours on jobs to afford college, his job as a bartender at Sadlacks, an infamous student-populated bar in Raleigh and the role of luck in a working stiff's life provided rich fodder for a long conversation. By the time the plane landed in Salt Lake City, we had thoroughly enjoyed each other's company and had a flyer for the local church pushed at us, by a lady seated in the row behind. She had probably heard the whole conversation and decided that we needed help, or salvation, or both.

I had to get to Park City the same night, to meet up with a few other athletes I knew. They showed me some spectacular running trails which went up ski trails. On the flatter terrain, there was an occasional rattlesnake to contend with, but that usually made for a good speed workout. The city was athlete friendly, with some great bike shops, good places to sit and read, and calming scenery all around. After the uninspiring flats of Florida, I was in heaven.

After training for a month at an altitude, and barely making the registration for Ultraman Canada on time, I found myself on a plane once again, this time headed to the airport in British Columbia, also the home of some of the most legendary triathletes in the world. When I arrived in Penticton, I had only a day to meet my crew, organize supplies and go to sleep, little realizing the magnitude of what I was about to attempt in the coming days.

At Ultraman, a crew was mandatory for every athlete as a large part of the race was not supported by volunteers. Unlike at Ironman races, the Ultraman had no traffic closures. Athletes typically loaded up their nutrition in the crew vehicle, stopping at their own pace to fuel, change, rest and recover. Since the distances were so great, it was not logistically possible to have volunteers. Most crews my fellow competitors had brought along were friends or family, because these races are almost a rite of passage. Since I knew no one that I could pay to travel with me or crew for me, the race director was kind enough to suggest a few names. The fact that I did not know the crew beforehand would turn out to be a huge disadvantage, as there was no time to build trust or familiarity. They did not know me and I did not know them.

Ultra(wo)man

I read somewhere how important it is in life not necessarily to
be strong ... but to feel strong.
—Chris McCandless in John Krakauer's *Into the Wild*

1 August 2009 was the hottest day that year in Penticton, BC. Two
dozen intrepid souls had undertaken the journey to Ultraman,
starting with a 10-km swim in Lake Skaha. The Okanagan valley was
bristling, radiating some combination of blue, brown and green, three
of my favourite colours in God's palette. I remember being excited
but completely detached from everything at the start. My mother had
injured her back several months earlier, rendering her bedridden.
This was a woman who woke up at 6 a.m. every morning, to tend to
the family and home while also successfully working on a business she
owned. To see her immobilized was a severe reality check and cause
for depression. It had affected my training and preparations adversely,
leaving a bitter taste in my mouth and a deep sense of discontent. I knew
I was not operating at my best. That was when I came across an athlete,
Jason Lester, who was missing an arm but appeared upbeat and happy.
This motivated me to stay calm and focused before the start of the race.

Once the gun went off, we had to navigate a point-to-point swim
with a kayak guiding us. Lori, one of my crew members, who happened
to be the best of the lot, was on the kayak, orienting me, as there were
no markers on the water. In a long-course swim, there is a huge element
of trust involved between the crew and the athlete. When in the water,
the swimmer cannot really see the end. Trusting the crew is tantamount

to success because they can see farther and act as eyes for the swimmer. I had some issues at the beginning trusting Lori, simply because I did not know her at all and I was eager to do well in the water. After the first stop to chow down some marble cake and coffee from the kayak, I decided that I was going to put my swim in her hands. It turned out to be a good bet. Lake Skaha and I made friends fast. The whole time, the lake seemed to be murmuring to me about love, support and happiness. We were swimming halfway across this huge lake and I was thinking about my journey in training that made this possible. Training for Ultraman Canada had involved a lot of strict choices and long hours. I thought about the ride to Nelson and an epic swim at the QE2, sans goggles. I had to trust my work ethic that day, just as I had to trust Lori to help me make it to the end of the swim.

Once out of the water, I quickly transitioned to my bike for the 150-km bike ride to Christie Beach, covering most of the Ironman Canada course. The bike course on the first day looped from Okanagan Falls, where the swim ended, over the Richter Pass and back to Okanagan. The ride started well, but the heat was unbelievable. I had no doubt that I was going to finish, but as time went on, I had to get off twice to avoid dizziness and nausea. I realized later that I should have kept myself cool with sponges and focused on my race, rather than chatting with the crew at every stop. I was talking too much, trying to get to know my crew. They seemed really moody and I just didn't get it. Jo Mead, the race marshal, saw that I was in trouble, 50-km from the finish. He handed me a big bottle of water and said, 'You can make it, kick some ass!' I knew I could make it even though I was suffering, but eventually, some drama unfolded. To be fair, these events are very hard on the crew, who have to drive and stop nearly every 10 km. In the last 40 km or so, my crew wanted me to stop and quit the race. They just did not think the heat was good for me. I shut them out as best as I could. I was no stranger to people doubting the abilities of women endurance athletes. I avoided pit stops like the plague in the last twenty or so kilometres, just so I did not have to talk to the crew or assimilate their negativity. Lori was trying to help me, but the others outnumbered her. I asked Jo to hand me water when he could because I was afraid my crew would stop me and take my bike away. Jo Mead turned out to be a gift to the misfits, waifs and strays of the world. At the end of day one, when I simply couldn't bring myself to share a room with the crew, he was kind enough to take me in and give me a room in the basement of his house. I crashed in his guest bedroom and slept badly.

Jo was a bit surprised when I woke up at 4 a.m. on the second day and insisted that he take me to Denny's, a local diner, to place an order for five milkshakes as nutrition for the 270-km bike ride that was the second stage of the race. While Jo could house me, it would not be possible for him to be my crew. I figured the less often I stopped, the less I would talk to anyone in my own crew, whom I was married to till the finish. Denny's supplied my nutrition along with blue crushed-ice Slurpies and Snickers bars. I started the day severely dehydrated. The crew chief and I decided to keep our issues out and work towards reaching the finish line. The ride started in Penticton and ended in Princeton with a lot of climbing. Since the previous day's bike ride had been staggered with swimmers coming out of the water at different times, I had no opportunity to take in the competition on the bike. When we were at the start line on day two, I quickly realized that my museum piece bike was quite the source of amusement to competitors, crew, and marshals alike. No one said anything rude, but there was some humorous jibing about my wheels, my not-so-aerodynamic aerobars and the peeling paint on the cranks. I took it all in my stride with much laughter because I knew that if I told anyone how ridiculous my old bike setup was, they would probably never believe me. Besides, I was wearing bike shorts with 'Brazil' written on them, accessorized with a nose-ring. The fashion police never particularly bothered me. I had finally scrounged together some money for that carbon bike frame in New Zealand. Carbon frames are lighter and more fun to ride, although any athlete worth their salt will tell you that in the absence of sponsors and after kicking back several miles, equipment matters least. I reused my old bike parts from Mrs Martinez in the carbon frame, so basically, it was a transplant. Same bike, different body.

When the ride started, I felt good for the first 100 km or so. Maybe after a good night's sleep, the crew felt better too. We talked briefly before the start and they seemed happy to help me by carrying my nutrition on the ride. The second day was just as hot as the first, with the added element of smoke in the air. Since I was focused on taking in my nutrition and as much of the scenery as I could, I did not notice the rise in temperature. The first day had been still throughout, which made the heat extremely unbearable. The second day was more varied and a little more fun as there was some wind to contend with. I love riding into a headwind, it brings out the best in me.

While the first day had about 4,000 feet of climbing, the second day had more than 5,000 feet and required a near-consistent effort throughout the ride. Right around 100 km, my sunglasses fell off. I was concerned, because this meant riding on a bright day with smoke residue from local wildfires in my contact lenses. My crew showed a lot of initiative in locating my glasses and handing them to me before the first big climb started. We climbed for nearly 27 km over 3,000 feet and there were plenty of false summits and tough rollers, but I was prepared for them from climbing the Lewis Pass. I could see that some of my competitors were literally melting. One lady got off her bike, cursed quite loudly, and started to cry. I would later find out that a lot of people suffered a great deal and ended up quitting. I had not bothered to check the elevation profile in any detail, so I was not expecting anything at all, good or bad. After a 25-km descent, we climbed another 100 km, this time more gradually ascending back to 3,000 feet. At first I felt smug knowing that I did not feel much discomfort. I thought of what Chris McCandless says in *Into the Wild:* '… and I know how important it is in life not just to BE strong but to FEEL strong.' I sure felt very strong. My nutrition plan was working perfectly. I had only stopped once to shove ice down my clothes as the salt had started to cake on my body. My simple helmet, with its multiple war wounds, was the best equipment choice I had made. It kept my head cool till the end, literally and figuratively.

The last 20 km of this 100-km climb really tested my resilience. As with most races, I was back on the sine wave of emotions, and cynicism began to set in. My chances of finishing seemed bleak because I was tiring out pretty fast. All my doubts came back to haunt me. Maybe everyone who had made fun of my bike that morning was right. Maybe my bike was a joke. Maybe Chris McCandless was overrated. Maybe Jon Krakauer made the whole thing up. Maybe my crew was right in discouraging me. Who did I think I was, anyway? Maybe I should pack it in and fly to New Zealand early. Maybe my advisor would kick me out of the lab, but he was not around much lately, so maybe the administrator would do the kicking. Maybe I was just deluded in thinking that I could even pull this off. Just as the avalanche of doubt washed over my entire body, reason kicked in. Wait, it said. My mother thought I could pull this off and my mother, annoyingly, is seldom wrong. My bike was named Blue Sambar and it could never go wrong because lentils were good for the muscles. My crew didn't matter because this was just a three-day love-affair gone wrong. Flying to New Zealand early on non-refundable, cheap flights was out of the question. My advisor's administrator was also never around, so being kicked out was unlikely. I perked up, if only momentarily, and decided to bring back positive memories.

The last 60 km of the ride were very rough on me, but all I could see and hear was my mother's face and voice. She was the only person who had told me all year, over and over, that I should start the race. Finishing was not important, starting was. She was the voice in my head and the wind on my back. I thought of my father, a seemingly silent force of life for me, understated as always, remembering to say 'best of luck' three times, without prompting, before I started this race.

That night, dinner was less tense. The crew had warmed up to me after Day 2, or so I wanted to believe. I still maintained a cautious distance because I knew I had a very long way to run the next day. I met a kid called Morgan from Central Canada who said he had been cheering for me from the first day. His parents were crewing for another athlete and he was along for the ride. That's the thing about Canadians:

they are so generous with their energy, time and love that you cannot help but feel that the odds are stacked in your favour. Morgan was shy at first, but kids are on my wavelength more than adults on any given day. We ended up chatting for a very long time and he promised to wait for me at the finish line. I did not have the heart to tell him my doubts and didn't think he would wait that long anyway.

I was ecstatic starting the run. I blew kisses to everyone at the start line and on the race course. There were good vibes in the air. Even the competitors were supportive in their messages. I took great pride in running alongside Kurt Becker, who was running on a severely injured foot. I had made a few friends by Day 3. Charlie, a university professor who had heard me describe my crush on legendary computer architect and mathematician from the Midwest, Seymour Cray, told me that Mr Cray would have been proud of me. I laughed to myself. That good ol' Minnesotans and the Midwest had given me everything I needed to survive: a big work-ethic and a hardy attitude. I didn't have the energy to talk much, but I heard every one of the positive messages, and I carry them with me even now. My troubles with the crew continued, though. When there was friction with them, I focused on the positives they brought to the table. There was Lori, my one true support on the kayak, who would even stand up to her best friends in my defence. They had picked me up at 1 a.m., when I landed in Penticton after several delayed connections. They had retrieved my sunglasses on Day 2, before I had started climbing 'The Wall'. Theirs was a thankless job – *Be grateful*, I said to myself. The best thing was to speak as little as possible. Wasting energy was not on my to-do list for the day.

After running around 43 km, I found myself in the company of the lovely Jody Michael, whose crew made me laugh my head off with their pom-poms and funky chicken moves. Jody had red socks on and a constantly kind word to share. Janet Holden, another competitor, who was keeping a good pace uphill, also kept me from getting run over by traffic by shielding me when I veered off the shoulder.

As the day progressed, however, the negativity from two people on my crew started to wear me down. Once again, they were not being helpful and I didn't understand it. I was simply running quietly. I had nothing much to say and I wasn't sure what I was expected to say, either. I knew my job was to keep my mouth shut and run. One of them was making notes on what I was eating, as she was aspiring to participate the following year, and trying to change my nutrition plan on the run. I was not in the mood to negotiate, because I knew what I needed to eat and I did not want anyone standing in my way. I asked them politely to leave me alone with just over 30 km to go. Even if I failed, I wanted to fail privately and not amidst sceptics screaming 'I told you so!' In the last 10 km, I met three people who contributed in volumes to my finishing. Lena, a volunteer and a previous winner, Amber, another volunteer, and Marvin Bolt, a competitor. Their optimism and reinforcement kept me from caving in. The cumulative dehydration, the massive stress resulting from lack of sleep and worrying constantly about support from my crew had taken its toll on me. Lena held my hand for nearly two kilometres, running alongside me, reminding me to never give up.

When I finished, my mind and body were completely spent. Morgan was right there at the finish line, as he had promised he would be. He tried frantically to make me comfortable and was close to tears, watching me suffer. That kid taught me about how a complete stranger can be invested in your success, with no expectations from you. I try to pay that forward as often as I can.

I remember shivering uncontrollably for ninety minutes. I remember the massage table coming to me. I remember piling into a car and checking into the emergency room for four rounds of IV before the doctor would let me go. I remember being alone in that hospital room, without a soul around me, feeling utterly miserable. I was all alone, and for the first time in a very long time, wishing that I was home to eat my mother's food and have her hold my hand. I remember smiling, thinking of the shirtless crews of the top athletes and very much appreciating the view. I remember the nurse looking at me with pity and incredulousness in equal measure. I remember thinking that it had taken a Canadian village to get an Indian to the finish line. I remember knowing, deep in my heart, that no coach, no guidance counsellor, no hero had gotten me there. My life then and now continues to be a series of modest episodes, while the seemingly ordinary people I am surrounded by demonstrate extraordinary heroism in their daily lives. These were the people who had gotten me there. My parents, the competitors, all the spectators on the course, one brilliant shirtless Brazilian who took a picture with me on Day 2 that scandalized my aunts to no end, and, of course, Lori.

At the awards ceremony the day after the Ultraman finished, I heard stories about how one competitor had not done any swimming until the last four weeks because it had been too cold in the UK to swim. I laughed thinking about that, recalling my own swim strategy before Ironman Brazil. I was proud of myself for keeping the negative voices out and focusing on the positive. It had taken a lot out of me, but I was happy about the final result, and my choices. Every minute in the ER and the big fat bill that followed was worth it. Luckily, I had bought health insurance for travel. I felt the music right before I fell asleep in the hospital, floating away to a land where the horizon glimmered with promise of faith and trust in the human element.

THROUGH THE LOOKING GLASS

Airwave

Follow a train of thought 'til
It leads you to your station
And everyone there is on time
No worry or fear will find you.
                    —Boh Runga, *Airwave*

I graduated in May 2010, eight months after Ultraman. My advisor called me one day and told me he thought I was ready to graduate, given my publications, and also encouraged me to shoot for the university record of graduating in twenty-six months with a PhD. He said it would be a good way to distinguish myself. I was touched. His faith meant the world to me. As it turned out, I had even more reason to be grateful to him for having pushed me to finish early because six months later, in November 2010, all hell broke loose. New Zealand was devastated by two earthquakes within six months of each other. The epicentre of the first earthquake was in Darfield, 40 km west of Christchurch. The second one, six months later, was an aftershock with its epicentre at Christchurch and a magnitude of 6.3. Most of the roads I loved running and cycling on, through the hills and the plains, were severely damaged and rendered too dangerous to traverse for a very long time. The swimming pool in which I had trained was swallowed up by the earth and then permanently closed. The beaches I had spent countless hours on, running, walking or dreaming at sunset, turned into safety hazards. We were in Christchurch that February, on our honeymoon and we saw first-hand how it changed the lives of the people living there, forever. Speaking of which, yes, I did find someone crazy enough to marry me.

When I returned to Bangalore after graduation, it seemed as though not much had changed. Except that the roads I biked on had even more construction work happening alongside them. However, my life took an entirely different turn when I was offered a faculty position at IIT Ropar, 70 km from Chandigarh, Punjab. I had felt a strong urge to teach for a while and I was fortunate enough to be given a chance to do just that. Teaching was a completely different experience, and it would contribute greatly to my evolving world-view. Especially in terms of understanding the disparities, which riding my bike for hundreds of miles could not teach me, and living the realities of rural India, as my parents had done many decades ago. I am often asked how to 'balance' life, and my answer has always been that there is no balance to be found – difficult pursuits often demand an unbalanced view of the world.

My first days as a teacher at IIT Ropar in June 2010 were some of the most beautiful days of my life. I had sought advice from my friends at Purdue, two of whom, Sunil and Shiva, were teaching at IIT Madras. Arriving in Rupnagar, I was very happy. The offices we were assigned had dragonflies as part-time tenants. I didn't mind. I was looking at the vast greenery past the campus gates, from my office windows. Fields of emeralds!

On my first day at work, I went to the administrator in charge of utilities to complain about my creaking worktable. I began by saying in my usual way, 'I have an issue.' He said, 'Oh, really! I had no idea. Records par to nahin hai, madam.' I said, 'What records? I just found out.' He looked taken aback and said, 'Oh...'

I was confused by his response, but before I could say anything more, we were interrupted by two other people who had more pressing matters for the utilities office to attend to. The toilets were not working. I stepped aside, puzzled, and called Sunil. 'Dude, what is the deal here?' I asked, unable to keep the bewilderment out of my voice. He asked me to describe the full conversation. I did. He burst out laughing. 'What did I do now?' I asked impatiently. He said, 'Anu, in government offices, "issue" refers to children.' Great! Here we go, I thought, another new place, another set of rules and things to familiarize myself with. I must be a glutton for punishment.

Within a few weeks though, I ceased to be bothered by the things that others found challenging – snakes on campus, drinking water problems, waterlogging. I quickly found a set of colleagues who had literally built the place up, the temporary campus being housed in what used to be a government girls' polytechnic, aptly painted pink. I had fun discovering the local haunts, admiring how brave some Punjabi women were, including the coach at a local pool in Chandigarh that I swam at, and discovering a completely new world within my own. The campus had a back gate that led directly to the banks of a canal of the Satluj River, but I wasn't confident about running there alone. So I formed a student group to run in the evenings. The first outing resembled a scene from *Chak De India*. It was hilarious. What was even more hilarious was when a guard quizzed one of my colleagues, Ashish, about the Delhi Half-Marathon; some of the students and Ashish were planning to run. The guard said, 'Sir, *suna hai aap bees kilometre bhaagne waale hain*?' (Sir, I heard you are running 20 kilometres.) Ashish replied, '*Haan ji*.' (Yes, sir.) The guard said, 'Sir, *paise kitne milte hain*?' (How much do you earn for running?) Ashish said, '*Paise milte nahin hain, dene padte hain, 500 rupaiye*.' (I don't earn anything, in fact I pay 500 rupees to enter the race.) At which the guard, with a look of total incredulity said, 'Sahab, 500 *rupaiye aap doge aur bees kilometre aap hi bhaagoge*?' (What! You pay 500 rupees and your run 20 kilometres?)

The students at IIT Ropar were more motivated than most and eager to learn. They brought the kind of joy into my daily life that I probably cannot aspire to find in entirety again. We had faculty from all parts of the country, my better friends being young people, daydreamers and idealists who allowed me to believe that one *can* make friends in later life.

Every morning, the faculty that was housed in Mohali would take a college-run transport service to get to the IIT on NH-21. Local wisdom had it that this highway had one of the highest accident rates in Punjab. Some blamed the temple that was on the way, because it made drivers take their hands off the wheel to pay their respects, some blamed drunk driving, but I think it had something to do with the sheer speed of the vehicles hurtling in all directions up and down the road. I would often catch myself daydreaming on that ride to work, admiring the millions of butterflies trying to cross the road. Punjab was green, green, green, and green happens to be my favourite colour. There were farms for miles on end and the scenery was no different from what I was used to in New Zealand, Seattle, Utah or Canada on my long rides, minus the accident rate, of course. The blue skies were remarkably optimistic, the job as visiting faculty was demanding, and we had to get through an interview to land a permanent job at the end of the semester, which meant working hard on both publications and teaching. I did not mind the long hours one bit. I swam before work, ran during lunch or in the evenings, and biked around my neighbourhood on the weekends. I had decided to take some time off from competing, plus a short sabbatical from my company. My body was in sore need of rest and it was time I listened to its plea for help. I had fallen several times on my left shoulder when writing my thesis, owing to some combination of sleep deprivation and spacing out into a world of equations at stoplights in Christchurch. I could not get the physiotherapy I needed to fix my shoulder then and I have not found it till today – sports medicine has a long way to go at home, in terms of being easily accessible.

Early on in my stay, I had run into Ashish, a very quiet man who handled the faculty recruitment and integration. On talking to him, I found out that he had lived in Austin for a while. In fact, we had been in the same building, on different floors, with a bit of a time-drift between his graduation and my arrival. 'What a small world we live in,' I said and laughed. Little did I know that it would close in even further, very soon.

When I thought about it, I knew that being neurotic and driven was not an appealing quality in a woman. I'd had my share of wonderful and really bad relationships. All in all, in love, I only knew what I did not want. I did not want a self-obsessed man. I did not want a manly man, who thought child rearing was a woman's job. I did not want a hypocrite, who expected a paycheque from me but did not expect to contribute himself. I did not want a pushover, a yes-man, or a momma's boy. I did not want someone who did not like to help out, in life, in decisions, in everything. A partnership, to my mind, had to be exactly fifty-fifty.

Not being obsessed with finding a partner was liberating in many ways. I knew I loved my freedom to explore the world with my own earnings and on my own two legs or wheels. That meant a lot to me and it still does. Besides, Aurora had a very straightforward formula. She said, 'Don't get crushes on ass*@$!s, please ... only the finest man for you, seven feet tall and eyes that could start a small fire.' That simplified my life greatly.

Ashish, his roommate and I became good friends. I heard about his incredible work ethic, saw it first-hand, and fell head over heels in love with him in no time. All the reasons I came up with about why a relationship with him was a very bad idea, professionally and otherwise, remained fleeting thoughts. As hysterically as I might laugh while watching a Karan Johar movie with its high-pitched drama around romance, I suddenly felt a kinship with that Punjabi man – the director, that is. Ashish was also Punjabi and someone with a great, if understated, resilience to life's curveballs. Punjabis suddenly seemed like people I could easily understand: the swim coach in Chandigarh, Ashish, and maybe, in a decade, even Karan Johar!

I knew very little about Ashish. I knew he liked Jay Sean and country music. I tried to create a deep psychological profile based on his choices in music, but I didn't get very far. I tried to make conversation around less official matters but given my extensive social skills, I ended up talking rubbish and was convinced at the end of it that he would think me insane, or lonely, or both. I was none of those things. I had plenty of friends. I was even making friends with the vegetable vendors at Kharar market. My life was just fine. But I could not stop wanting to talk to the man. The fact that he kept asking me out for very platonic lunches did not help matters. I desperately wished for a filter between my brain and my mouth – not to mention my phone. It was one of those out-of-body experiences where I watched myself desperately shouting at myself to stop, but some kind of verbal diarrhoea kept taking over. I knew it was pointless to deny my feelings. I was definitely not interested in marrying anyone at that point, but that's the thing about life – it doesn't wait around for your insecurities to evaporate.

To escape myself, I ended up running away to the Philippines to compete in a race. It was the only place I could afford to go on my visiting professor salary. I had not trained much and was severely sleep deprived when I arrived in Manila.

Once there, I was finally able to breathe. I planned a quick trip on landing, to get a bite to eat and visit a very special place. As I stood in the foyer of the hotel I was staying in, waiting for the taxi to arrive, I could hear Ashish's favourite Jay Sean being played loudly. I wondered if the universe was getting back at me for laughing at my buddy who had proposed marriage to me when I was still a graduate student in Raleigh. I will never forget the song that was playing in the loo that day – *'Two less lonely people in the world'*. I wondered if I was simply clueless.

It took seventy-five minutes to get to Quezon city from my ramshackle hotel near the airport and my driver Tefilio and I quickly became great friends. He had two daughters, roughly my age. We were headed to Quezon City, to the Araneta Coliseum, where the '"thrilla" in Manila', the famous fight between Joe Frazier and Muhammad Ali, took place in 1975. I wanted to go there to see what it looked like and to think about what sport meant to me at this point, something of a question-and-answer-solo-trip. After paying a guard a hundred pesos to sneak into the Coliseum, I sat down for a while on the bleachers and thought about my journey so far. I was not afraid of anything. I had been disappointed by my experiences in Madison as a PhD student the first time around. People around me had preached one thing, practised another. My parents, who by example inspired me to choose a path of independence both financially and emotionally, had uplifted me. I had recovered nicely and then, as a reward, life had thrown me a different bone: sport.

My company was doing well. There were no investors, no sugar-daddies and no dependencies. I had earned my keep and I had earned it well. Getting a PhD in New Zealand had been a homecoming of sorts. Life in research had been enjoyable, especially the company that surrounded me in my lab, the engineers, designers, artists, scientists. I no longer envied those beautiful women from liberal arts at Purdue, or anywhere else. I felt rested, knowing that enjoyment was a basic tenet of success and inspiration. My advisors in New Zealand had been ethical, they had enjoyed seeing a woman succeed. I believed I was treated equally and sometimes better than my male counterparts. One of my advisors was American, one Kiwi, and one Sri Lankan. Love knows no geography. Neither do ethics and encouragement. Neither does merit. I had worked hard in academia. It was only circumstantial, which end of the wave I caught with failure or success.

Sport itself had taken me to unexpected places. The average professional athlete trained 25-30 hours a week. For four years, I averaged that volume, on my own terms, without anyone funding me. I visited repeatedly the dwelling of my inner goddess, the forests, and ran free. I was most proud of that.

The reason to engage in sport had evolved over time. Training in India for my first Ironman had been a wonderful adventure, a curiosity-driven experiment. A great girly secret between my mother and me. The second race had been a less wonderful adventure, with the pollution catching up to me. The races after that, leading up to Ultraman, had been my path to the pursuit of excellence, both physical and mental. On the flight to the Philippines, I had watched a movie where the villain asked the heroine (whom he was in love with), 'Does your god feel jealous?' I felt jealous of people who spoke casually about how hard their life was, when in fact they had no idea what hardship meant. I hoped I did not end up in that category – I wanted to seek out gratitude and appreciate all that was available to me, in the best and worst of circumstances. My present time in Manila was a privilege, any day of the week, not to be confused with anything else and never to be taken too seriously. I was not in danger of being controlled by the demands of longer equipment lists and fancier races, as far as sport was concerned. I loved sport, had excelled in it to my own modest measure and I planned on continuing to participate, shaping my dreams to fit my shoes and my train of thought. Truly loving something can be articulated by the lyrics from the song 'Hotel California': 'You can check out any time you like, but you can never leave.'

Oblivious to the odds or not, I had a lot to be happy about. I was working hard and my heart was doing lunges at the speed of light, but the fact that I could do what I wished to, even if it was running away from the boy I was falling for, was a privilege. One I was deeply grateful for. I convinced myself that Ashish was just a random crush, to be included alongside other brain farts. Love was not as simple as sport.

My flight to Naga was the following morning, at the unearthly hour of 6 a.m. For three days I had been waking up at around 2.30 a.m. India time, which was good for race-prep and setting my body clock, on hindsight. On landing, we were welcomed by a bunch of dancers and an amazing view of the Isarog shrouded in clouds. I was in love. I had the best crew I could have asked for to help me. Asian races are really first-class events. Anyone can tell you that. I had a flight out of Naga after the race ended at 3.20 p.m., the same day. I thought, given my present chubby-tubby, untrained, orangutan-like condition, it was very unlikely that I would finish the race. I was bargaining for the swim, bike and one loop of the run as I had a midterm to give to my students on Wednesday and I did not want to lose my job by taking a later flight.

The swim was amazing, the bike ride was superb, but the run was a death-march. On the bike, we were not alone for even a split second. There were so many children and bands cheering in the hot, hot sun that I could not help smiling, laughing and having a great time. I got through the ride in three hours and twenty minutes, twenty minutes worse than my personal best, and I figured this had something to do with my not riding the bike for over three months. Stupid boys; always time-consuming. I heard a lot of 'Beautifool eendian woman, marry me,' and I thought, 'Wow! This whole place loves me, there is no good reason to frown.' Additionally, I had a lot of confused thoughts about

Ashish's message, which had reached me after I boarded the flight to Manila out of New Delhi. 'Run like the wind,' it said. I knew Indian men were very hard to please, read and understand, so I knew I had to finish the run to impress him, or at the very least, the first lap to impress myself. I thought a lot about stopping after the first lap, but there seemed to be no good reason to do so. I was well in time for my flight and I wanted that medal to show the boy. Also, there were plenty of brown, beautiful babies to high five and I couldn't disappoint my to-be in-laws, should I marry that Filipino who had proposed on the race course. I only got competitive once, when this annoying woman said something like, 'I was so happy when you were behind me ... grunt ... now you are ahead of me ... grunt...' I wanted to tell her, 'Honey, I haven't seen my shoes except in the last three weeks and my bike in three months and I have a plane to catch. Besides, my grunts are way better than yours.'

I ran right through the finish line to the hotel lobby, took a quick shower, changed my clothes, and was on a bus to catch my flight within fifteen minutes of finishing the race. The race organizers were instrumental in ensuring that my bike was packed and ready to go by the time I got into the lobby and they made sure I had my taxi too.

My life came full circle once I returned from Manila. Turned out, Ashish had suffered a major heat stroke as the monsoons were delayed and we were an item before I knew it, strolling along the banks of a canal behind our campus or Pinjore garden. We mostly talked about our families, what we found cool about Austin, programming languages and other geeky subjects. When I called my father to discuss Ashish and possibly getting serious with him, the conversation went like this:

Me: 'Father, I might be dating a new boy.'

Father: 'Good, good, is he good to you?'

Me: 'Yes. I might want to marry him.'

Father: 'Hmm ... Is this about your aunts? Have they been calling you? Listen, just ignore them. Your periamma Sacchu will have my head if I pressure you.'

Me: 'No one calls me, Father. I don't pick up the phone, remember?'

Father: 'Okay. You want to marry him? I probably will have to see it to believe it. Does he want to marry you?'

Me: 'I hope so.'

Father: 'Well, find out first, then call me.'

And he hung up.

We were married in December, in Swamimalai. We received five copies of the book *Two States: The Story of My Marriage*, but our parents were more than happy. My father was rather shocked in a bewildered, adorable way, like he still couldn't quite believe that his daughter was getting married.

Marriage was nothing like I expected, because I didn't know what to expect to begin with. I was clear that it was not going to be a Bollywood movie, so was he. Fairytales are overrated in my book. We faced plenty of challenges as I decided to turn down the full-time position even after clearing the dreaded interview and moved to Ahmedabad with Ashish, where he started work towards another degree while I taught new classes. Ahmedabad had its own peculiar problems, but once again, this was one of the most beautiful parts of my life. After a few years, looking forward to the birth of our first child, I was finally sure that waiting for true love had been entirely worth it. Maybe I got lucky, but come on, Ropar, Punjab was the last place where I had expected to find my partner.

Tramp

The moon is most happy when it is full,
the sun always looks like a perfectly minted gold coin
polished and placed in flight by God's playful kiss.
And so many varieties of fruit hang plump and round.
I see the beautiful curve of a pregnant belly
shaped by a soul within,
and the earth itself.
I have gotten the hint:
There is something about circles the Beloved likes.
Within the circle of a Perfect One
there is an infinite community of light.

—Hafiz (1325-1389), *Circles*

O ne of the questions I have grown to dread as a working mother is, 'Where are you from?' Where am I from? Am I from Safdarjung Avenue, New Delhi, where I was born? Am I from Bangalore, where I was raised? Am I from the Midwest, where I learned how to work hard to eke out an honest living? Am I from North Carolina, where I fell in love with forests that reignite my will to live, no matter how dire the circumstances? Am I from Madison, where I learned the value of self-respect? Am I from a Tamilian household, where women are treated equal to men and their capabilities never doubted? Am I a Kiwi, because it was in New Zealand that I learned the joy of training hard without desiring the glory? Am I from my mother-in-law's house, where I was blessed with the wisdom of her culture and mine? Where *am* I from? I have no clue, really.

I believe women find themselves at many more crossroads than men do, requiring us to constantly re-evaluate what we hold closest to our hearts, at different points in time. Going from being an engineer to completing Ultraman Canada, undertaking a 10-km swim, 420-km bike ride and 84.4-km run while working towards a PhD was not my life-long ambition. It was a milestone reached after hours of hard work, labouring towards a goal only I could see. I did not care for consensus and often followed my heart, even when my head got in the way. I was determined; resolve was a big part of my identity and my conversation with life. It would be safe to say that I have always espoused extremes, to the point of being unbalanced, as most pursuits towards excellence are.

When I became pregnant, I had to re-evaluate my relationship with my body. I ran and swam for the first four months or so, but after that, all I could do was walk. My determined self reared its head when I took up walking as an endurance sport. I often walked an hour before breakfast, and several hours in the early afternoon or evening. Walking, unlike triathlon training, gave me long stretches of time to think. Admittedly, it was a little intimidating at first.

On one such walk with my husband, when I was twenty-eight weeks pregnant, on what would be one of our last trips before the baby was born, we found ourselves in a town called Bingen, in Germany. We had decided to attempt walking as much as we could, from Bingen to Koblenz, a 70-km stretch on the banks of the Rhine. The Rhine is a north-flowing river and I took this walk to symbolize a celebration of the two people walking it.

On a map, the route from Bingen to Koblenz looked like a tick-mark. My husband had biked this route with a motley crew, at speeds not worth mentioning, many moons ago. He wanted me to see how beautiful it was. We arrived at Bingen late in the afternoon, walking an hour to get a feel of the trail towards Rudensheim and back, a total of 10 km. This was in the middle Rhine valley, which was overflowing with cyclists and walkers. That particular weekend was cold, but stunning. The foliage was just beginning to show and we were glad for the milder temperatures, as anything hotter would have meant more rapid dehydration and more stops.

Walking for an hour or two is quite different from walking all day, as I discovered on that trip. My husband has a quiet and beautiful mind, housed in the body of a lissome runner, with an unusually imaginative take on life. He loves walking, and I loved the fact that we could share an activity besides reading and long conversations. Having running or cycling as your primary on-ground activity can be very limiting when it comes to including your partner, if he happens to be the geek you cannot imagine your life without.

The first day of all-day walking, or tramping as it's called, we set off at 8 a.m., hoping to avoid the morning chill while getting an early enough start. We had plenty of time to take in the details on the first stretch of around 22 km, our final destination being Oberwesel. Armed with a backpack full of water and food, my trusty iPod that was not to be turned on barring an absolute mental breakdown, a credit card and a change of clothes, we felt pretty chipper for most of the way. This particular trail is dotted with castles and poplars and London plane trees.

Being a tramp is serious business. One needs to master the art of falling asleep, wherever, whenever, however. It's an art I find most difficult to practise at home. But we were not trying to set any records, mostly looking forward to spending time together and accomplishing what would be a reasonably challenging physical feat. My belly was singing a happy tune, and I thought our baby would grow up to be pretty happy outdoors. Maybe green would be a favourite colour in the family for some time to come.

The trail was marked by several towns along the way. On the first day of walking all day, we crossed places named Assmanhausen, Lorch and Bacharach, which made me giggle. Walking with anyone over an extended period of time teaches you a lot about that person. What they talk about, how they structure their thoughts, how they handle the inevitable low of exhaustion and, most of all, their perspective on the world and its many happenings.

After a quick stop for lunch during the day and several sit-downs to rub my feet, take in the sights or both, we arrived at Oberwesel, 22 km later. I smiled thinking about how tramping made the world appear so much clearer. I remember going to bed content and excited about the second day. We had covered more than 32 km, including our little jaunt on the evening we arrived in Bingen. We were ready to sleep. The compression socks and comfort iPod also rested, with more work to do the next day.

Within the first few kilometres of walking on the third day, I was tired. Luckily for us both, the Lorlei rock was a milestone we had in mind and that kept me going. Visible from the western shore, along which we were walking, this rock rises well above the shoreline and has heavy currents, boat accidents and a feminine spirit associated with it. In 'Die Lorlei', a poem by Clemens Bartano, Lorlei is portrayed as an enchanting woman sitting atop the rock, distracting shipmen with her beauty, causing accidents and misadventures. That the point is also the narrowest part of the river and a sharp turn probably had a lot more to do with the misfortune of the mesmerized shipmen, but mythology can often be impervious to fact.

As we walked along, we talked about Adi Sankara, who walked all over India. We talked about Marco Polo, who also travelled great distances and balanced two diverse cultures in his head. We talked about Genghiz Khan, riding all over the steppe on his horse, and wondered if he ever sang softly to himself at Avraga. We talked about Xuanzhang, who escaped China unnoticed. I quickly realized that these were mostly men we were talking about. What about the women? Did Avvaiyar walk for seven hours before penning the verse 'Bend but do not break' in the *Aatichoodi*? In any case, brevity seemed to be directly proportional to enlightenment. Thiruvalluvar and his kurals. Avvaiyar and her *Aatichoodi*. The humble haiku, origins unknown to me. How did Avvaiyar feel about a cup of coffee to warm her hands? I could only wonder. We definitely see a lot of women who work in the fields, several months pregnant, sometimes giving birth there. Where are their voices when we talk about human endurance?

By the time we reached Sankt Goar, my hope had turned into desperate soreness. I was mad at myself for slowing my husband down. He was amused at my expectations from myself. The iPod did its bit for ten short minutes, before we sat down for lunch. I was too tired to appreciate the food. It was not as tasty as I had imagined it would be, having walked over 42 km over two days with my football-sized attachment. When we got up to leave, I caught a second wind. I think my husband's presence and voice helped more than the iPod had before lunch. We saw an old couple along the way, sitting hand in hand at a coffee shop. She was eating pistachio ice cream and he was drinking a beer. I was momentarily unable to take my eyes off them.

Maybe the second day aged us both in a nice way, for we were full of compassion for each other's aches and pains after another slow, long day of walking. Another 21 km later, we found ourselves in a little town called Boppard, where we stopped for the third night. There was some kind of gathering in the town and the inn owner was absent the next morning, leaving all his trekking guests in the lurch. When he finally showed up, which I can only imagine he did at some point, most of us had eaten breakfast elsewhere and left.

While we originally planned to get to Koblenz, I knew that I was physically too tired to go on by the time we approached a town called Spay, on the fourth day. We cut our walk short, covering a distance of 66 km, and spent the evening swapping notes about our fathers, both rather handsome and amazing men. We hoped the good-looking gene would not skip a generation, for our child's sake!

I had formed quite a few lasting memories over the years, tramping through Bangalore, Madras, Manali, Ahmedabad, Ropar, Mandi, Kovalam, Hyderabad, Tanjavur, Madurai, Aathoor and then through Illinois, California, Texas, North Carolina, Seattle, Christchurch, Auckland, Wellington, Wanaka, Coventry, Canberra, Beijing, Barcelona, the Rhine Valley and some other places I might have forgotten. They would come back to me, I was sure. Tramping through those places with my trusty running shoes and some spare change had added perspective to my world. I didn't give it all up like Alexander

Supertramp (Chris McCandless' trail-name), but I felt his hunger to be free for a large part of my life. Past all the busy and important titles, degrees and bank balances, I felt closest to this freedom while running, walking or most importantly, just being.

Giving birth brought with it a moment of great clarity. There was magic beyond what any class in engineering, science or objective observation had taught me. However, to sustain that magic past the endorphin rush of birth would involve a great deal of humility, I knew. To be able to bend my determined head, hold out my hands and say, *I am ready to allow this magic into my life.* Overnight, I went from being someone's daughter to being someone's mother. The transition was not lost on me.

Six weeks postpartum, my determination reared its head again and I decided I had to get out of the house and re-engage with the athlete in me. Having emotionally blackmailed my parents, who were with us for eight weeks after the baby was born, to travel down to a 10-km race, I handed our newborn to Grandma and set off towards the start line, hand in hand with my husband.

'I am not sure I can finish,' I said to him.

'Uh-huh', he replied.

'I am not sure my body is ready.'

'Uh-huh.'

'What if I am not able to finish?'

'Uh-huh.'

After a few iterations of the many doubts that plagued my mind, he suggested in the kindest possible manner that I should attempt the 5-km run, held on the same day, and build on that. I rolled my eyes and thought how clichéd men were and told him rudely, 'Five kilometres is not good enough, I am running all of it. That's that.'

I let go of his hand and ran to the start line, fuming. By the time I finished 3 km, my life flashed in front of my eyes. I had clearly not recovered from giving birth. I was moving slowly. I was embarrassed. On finishing the first 5 km, I saw my father on the sidelines. I walked over to him, mad at myself for doing so. I had always treated races as a test against time. To take walk breaks, that too on a 10-km race, was unimaginable. I told him I was not sure if I could finish. To this he said, 'Anu, I am having great fun watching your husband feed your baby, but think about it – not many men would agree to do this. Whether you finish or not, know that you made a start and your family was there to cheer you on.'

Encouraged by his words, I started running again. I knew I would take a minimum of seventy minutes and I was beginning to get embarrassed again, when a young boy on a bike pulled up next to me. He was shepherding the last few runners and this thought embarrassed me even more. But, talking to him, I realized that he wanted me to finish. He was cheering me on, although I was a complete stranger to him. That made me smile and I picked up my stride a little because it brought back such positive memories of my early involvement in sport.

I decided around the 8-km mark that I was done with the first version of me that was super-prepared and ready for every race and every battle. I was also done with the self-doubt that sometimes kept me from starting races and at other times kept me from finishing them. I wanted to finish this run, just for the pleasure of having my son know that his mother embraced life's challenges. I finished the 10 km, even though I could barely walk back to my family soon after.

I hope our child will someday see the value in dreaming, pursuing goals that are meaningful without flashbulbs, trophies, flowers or wine and that he will understand the nature of persistence. That being haunted by purpose, which does not control you, is not such a bad thing. And that (s)he who lasts the longest often gets to spots that are off the map, and they help us understand the changing nature of our relationship with our identity.

Epilogue

In deciding on the title of this book, I read an entire dictionary in one day. I thought I might title it *Strive* to evoke the idea of reaching further, higher, faster. That sounded like a self-help book though, and given that I can hardly help myself on most days, I did not think I was qualified to write a book on the subject. The second title that came to mind was *Higher Ground* – you know, like that UB40 song? While levitation is the trademark of every protein-ingesting triathlete, I did not think that was the focus of the book either. I ended up sticking to my original title, which was *Anywhere but Home,* because, to be honest, it seemed to me that I was perennially on a walkabout, seeking something just beyond reach. The image that comes to mind when I think of my various pursuits is of my looking into a warm living room, from the outside, wondering whether that is my home.

When I first researched endurance athletics, I was totally dumbstruck by the stories. The English Channel, which was a major trade route between ports in Roman Gaul and Britain as early as 55 BC, has historically attracted several crossings by sea and air. The record for swimming across the 32-km long and narrow waterway stands at around seven hours.

The Tour de France was initiated circa 1903, as a five-day stage race starting and ending in Paris, with stops at Lyon, Marseille, Bordeaux and Nantes, totalling over 2,100 km. While the early tours were open to whoever wished to compete, private participation was banned after 1930. However, the more colourful stories of how these private entrants, called *touriste-routiers,* made their way in the early editions of the epic race, often hustling to afford accommodation in the absence of professional team support, embodied the spirit of adventure. Presently the tour covers around 3,200 km and is rife with scandal owing to the meteoric rise in prize money.

The modern-day marathon was born from the legend of Pheidippides, a messenger who delivered a scroll brought from Marathon to Athens in a time of war. Between 1896 and 1921, the marathon was standardized as an Olympic sport. While the inclusion of women followed a more circuitous route and took nearly five decades, women have been part of the endurance community for a long time.

Katherine Switzer, who ran the Boston Marathon in 1967, was tackled by Jock Semple (the race director) since the arcane rules had not yet been updated a year later to include women.

Ultramarathons probably trace their inception to long, unassisted hikes. For example, the Badwater Ultramarathon was born after a successful hike in 1969 by Stan Rodefer, across the salt flats in Death Valley. In his epic book, *Born to Run,* Chris McDougall also talks about the proclivity of women towards endurance sport and time and again, this finds examples in the endurance sport community. There is Diana Nyad, who swam for nearly fifty-three hours across the 177-km Florida Straits; Sister Madonna Buder, who holds the record for the oldest woman to complete an Ironman at age seventy-five, having started the sport at the age of forty-eight and long been a chain smoker; and Priscilla Welch, who took up running at a late stage and competed in marathons with some stellar times until age forty.

As I read more about long-course triathlon, I realized that the early adopters in Ironman were a lot like me. Sure, they were not college brats, but what stuck with me was that they were not rich or entitled. The story that stood out was that of Scott Molina, who won the Hawaii Ironman in 1988. Apparently, he worked in a burger joint, stocked shelves at a liquor store and was a swim coach, while training many, many hours himself to make a name in the sport. There were many stories of him riding clunky old bicycles in training, dressed in his mom's old sweaters. The athleticism of Molina and other early adopters like him seemed to go beyond the aspect of physical effort. They valued freedom, the right to define their challenges without the tyranny of being on the right path, wearing the right equipment and on the right bike.

As do I.

Acknowledgements

Writing this book has taken me back through many years of my life, reading old journals and letters, calling friends in the middle of the night to make sure I was remembering things correctly. To my friends Aurora, Derek, Peter, Sam, David, Rowan, George, Varada, Scott, and ten dozen others, I owe my life's greatest experiences.

I have had the good fortune of being surrounded by the right set of people to help me tell this story. My editor, Karthika V.K. at HarperCollins India, who gave me a chance I so poorly deserved, stands out in my mind. To get under the skin of the story I was trying to write and encourage me to produce the best version of it was her greatest gift to me. The entire team at HarperCollins Publishers India has been a treat to work with, answering my many questions patiently, especially Ajitha G.S., Vinithra Madhavan-Menon, Sameer Mahale and Amrita Talwar. My brothers Amit and Arun were silent witnesses to my work. My second mother Saroj and father Suresh-Chander, your blessings mean the world to me.

Many people suffered through the reading of multiple versions of this draft. Dean Karnazes took the time to read it and talk to me around Christmas and motivate me in more ways than one. Manu Joseph encouraged me by reading my draft and has inspired a new beginning. My husband Ashish spent many weeks before and after work, helping me clarify thoughts, sentences, words and commas – his eye for detail is unmatched, as is his desire to see me through difficult deadlines. A girl should be so lucky. My bikes Zippy, Blue Sambar and Mrs Martinez, you were my rainbows in all kinds of storms.

For Shiva, Shasta, Vivek, Alexandria, Nicholas, Julie, Kavya, Anuradha, Anamika, Mythili, Gireesh, Shantanu and Rajesh, who gave up precious family time so this book could come to life, I reserve my deepest gratitude.

For my mother Alamelu and father Vaidyanathan, no words can ever capture your greatest gift to me – the ability to laugh at situations and at myself and tide over almost anything.

For our son Aadi, life is so much better with you in it, kanna.